A
FROG HOLLOW
CHILDHOOD

A Memoir of Hartford

LYNN DAVIS

PAGE PUBLISHING, INC.
New York, NY

First originally published by Page Publishing, Inc. 2019

ISBN 978-1-64462-054-0 (Paperback)
ISBN 978-1-64462-055-7 (Digital)

Printed in the United States of America

Dedicated to my beloved mother and grandmother.

Contents

Introduction

The twenty-two chapters presented in this memoir represent a snapshot of my early years spent in the Frog Hollow section of Hartford, Connecticut, in the late 1940s and throughout the 1950s. They focus mainly on the routines of my childhood from kindergarten through eight years of grammar school, the oft-repeated rituals that cement one's memories. It is the curious fact of memory that whereas routines and rituals of childhood are often repeated over and over, they come through consolidated from the many to create one. The chapters are independent of each other, stand-alone, and the selection of which went first and which last was decided in part by tying in similar themes and time of year. The chapters connect insofar as some refer to episodes and routines covered in a different one.

I am grateful to family, relatives, friends, city archives, school, hometown sites, and my own recall that helped me write this memoir. I am also thankful for the Brownie camera that captured my early life and left its snapshots in family albums waiting for me to study to help me fill in this childhood recollection. The conspicuous fact in documenting my early years is how delightful they were and how much I miss those times.

The Ice, Coal, and Cash-Pay-for-Rags Men Came

I n the late forties and early fifties, I met three men whose work routines added fun to my childhood. The memories connected with their simple work have remained way beyond the last time I saw them in those years before my teens. Not only my grandmother and mother, but I, too, had a hand in their work.

I called the three the ice, coal, and cash-pay-for-rags men. Their work is no longer done in Connecticut, unless in the back of beyond somewhere, but was once done in the Frog Hollow neighborhood of Hartford where first I met them some summer or winter day in my youth.

Although the refrigerator began displacing the icebox in the 1920s, the iceman still delivered ice in the '40s and '50s because change came slowly to Hungerford Street, and many of us still needed a service that was then disappearing.

We'd put in the front living room bay window of our second-floor tenement flat a cardboard sign that read ICE in big, bold, black letters to inform the iceman that we required a stop on his rounds. He came a couple of times a week, depending on the weather and how fast the blocks melted in our icebox.

He drove up Hungerford in a big truck. Its sides were built of wooden laths holding in place piled high blocks of ice, like gigantic ice cubes, that dribbled a watery trail. It seemed every neighborhood kid and I were around.

He followed a work routine we knew by heart. He got out of the truck and walked to the back of it, ignoring the bunch of us watching from a distance.

That tall burly man easily stabbed an ice block with a large wooden-handled single-curved pick, dragging the dripping block to the edge of his truck. Then, clasping and trapping the ice block between the pointed tips of a double tong, he turned from the truck, flinging the ice onto his back and onto the long black rubber apron he wore to protect his clothes from the dripping cold block.

We weren't forgotten in his routine. "You kids stay off the truck, you hear? I'll be blamed if you fall and break your necks."

We heard but didn't listen. We waited our chance to pick up and grab loose ice the minute he jabbed the tongs into the sleek dripping block and made his way to our flat.

Bent under the icy load, he disappeared into our backyard and up the back hall stairway to the second floor that opened onto a huge kitchen typical of the 1897 brick tenements. He deposited the block into the icebox where it would remain until melted, absorbing heat from the warm surroundings but staying cold until melted down through the back of the box to a holding pan. The pan of aluminum, the width and length of the box and located under it, caught the melting ice which, if not emptied, overflowed.

Before the iceman came, my mother emptied and then scoured the holding pan and box. And, when the block disappeared, she prepared everything again for another ice block to replace the puddle in the pan. According to her, not even an iceman should see a dirty box.

The second floor of our tenement got hotter than the others, wedged the way it was between the first and third floors. I made my own air-conditioning by swinging the top box door with the ice in it back and forth, fanning myself in the released cold air. When Mom yelled, "Close the door; you're melting the ice," I slammed it shut.

Downstairs we, kids, listened for the iceman's return. If we couldn't grab ice chunks from the truck by standing on the street, we hopped onto the truck to scoop up the pieces to slurp later when he drove off. We used those pieces to cool our faces and quench our thirst in the endless, sweltering summers of childhood that seemed to play themselves out under a perennial sun.

Back when the iceman came, work was simple, like the icebox itself. The no-maintenance refrigerators of today know what they're doing without help from us. But the fun is gone.

The iceman wasn't the only one who came. Once upon a time, in the days when Chapel or Jackson were part of a phone number, there came the coal man. With a big burlap bag slung over his back, he reminded me of Santa Claus. But the coal man carried not gifts but shiny black nuggets to feed the iron furnace my grandmother owned. Through a low-screened window on the left side of the house the coal man unlatched, he dumped the coal onto a chute into the house's cellar. Each piece of coal tumbled down, making a black pile and turning up dust like tiny coal clouds before settling down within a doorless wood bin in a dark corner.

The cellar ran the length of the tenement house. How often the coal man filled the bin, I don't remember, but my grandmother, like my mother who panicked when the ice block got too small, also worried when the coal pile shrank.

I went to the musty dirt floor cellar to watch my grandmother tend the furnace. Each tenant had a "room" there, and our "cellar room" was to the left of hers. But she, as the landlady, had the largest in the middle. The stout black iron furnace stood left inside her "room" and the bin with the coal straight ahead under the only window.

Using my nickname, she warned, "Stand over there, Mammy girl, and don't get burned."

I watched her shovel the coals from the pile which, in long cold spells, disappeared as fast as a chunk of ice on a hot sidewalk. She teased the coals to life with small pieces of wood or newspaper. I stood far enough away as Grandmother poked with one of several long iron utensils inside the open mouth of the black iron furnace until it burned red hot like a sore throat. Then, with a thick rag to protect her hands, she slammed the stout door shut and pulled down on a heavy lock fitting. She put the stoker back into a holder it shared with several others, and the heat rose in its mysterious way from furnace to the white painted iron radiators found in each of the six big rooms of Grandmother's first-floor flat.

Other times, she opened a tiny door at the bottom of the furnace and poked the embers with a long black iron piece with a curved end to gather the cold gray ashes, which she dumped into a tin bucket. She let me help her with the dead ashes, knowing I wouldn't get burned. The small furnace door at the bottom, holding its residual ashes and embers, reminded me of the holding pan that caught the melted ice in our icebox.

The simple visible mechanics that made things work then required more labor but brought people together, like my grandmother and me, sharing the work. Gas and oil furnaces, which replaced the iron coal ones, run maintenance-free today. There's nothing much for any of us to do now to keep warm but plug in or switch on.

If the ice and coal men's jobs were fading in the forties and fifties, the cash-pay-for-rags man's routines were already on the periphery, more anachronistic and disappearing from Hartford's streets when I saw him one summer day. I heard the *clip, clop, clip, clop* of his dusty horse-drawn wagon as he came slowly down Hungerford. He pulled up in front of our houses to peddle his wares, shouting in a slow cadence as if to make the phrase last as long as he could and reach as many of his customers as possible. "Cash pay for rags. Cash pay for rags." We called him by what he said and did, the cash-pay-for-rags man. He dressed in his shabby trousers and shirt and wore a floppy hat to discourage the sun and clamped a pipe between his teeth. He, his horse, and a wagon filled with a plethora of wares, all blended in differing shades and shapes from cloth to tin wear. From his wagon, a mobile combination of flea market and goodwill store, he traded in clothing and household items. His business was to barter with his customers to get the best price for himself.

The peddler slowly climbed down from the wagon, turned to it, and lifted from the seat an iron weight that was flat on the bottom and rounded at top to which he had fastened a thick rope tied round an iron loop on top. He put the weight near the sidewalk curb. The wagon and horse would go nowhere until the old peddler was ready.

My grandmother, me in tow, hurried to the wagon that day and picked out a big piece of cloth she freed from the tangle of rags and wares. The cloth looked like one she used to open and close the furnace door. They haggled the price, the old woman and older man, both deft in the business of bartering. Finished with my grandmother, he pulled up his iron street anchor, mounted the wagon again, and with a *cliz, cliz* to his horse, moved down the street to other customers.

They were all gone one day, the ice, coal, and cash-pay-for-rags men, and I continued my later years without them. But they're there, in a memory diorama, to conjure up and entice down Hungerford Street once more in the Frog Hollow section of Hartford to our three-family brick tenement house to serve us in a summer sun or winter wind.

Hammonasset by Bus

Mom and Dad never learned to drive, so we never had a car. What luck! If we had a car, I wouldn't have had the adventure of going to Hammonasset Beach by bus. And I would insist on the experience again had I my life to live over.

Every sunny Sunday, my mother, father, sister, grandmother, and I got ready for the hour-and-a-half trip to the Connecticut shore. Grandma and Mom made sandwiches, packed fruit, dessert, and anything else we needed for a day spent in the sun and salt water. Grandma covered the food over with a tablecloth. A woven picnic basket with a solid wood lid and two carry handles held everything.

To complement the food stock, there required a plethora of items for a beach day, which included our travel clothes—from sandals and white oxford tie shoes (which Mom kept spotless with shoe polish), sunsuits and pedal pushers, to sunglasses and hats. Grandma always wore a flowered print dress and sturdy black tie shoes. She carried a pocketbook half the size of a beach bag. Besides a pail and sand shovel, my sister and I took toy boats, she a small one and I a larger wooden one with a sail put up when I launched it.

Before two of our trips in the late 1940s ended, Mom and Dad photographed our excursions, which began on the front porch at 119–121 Hungerford Street. The first set of pictures showed us without sunglasses, and the second, Dad, Mom, and I, with them. It must have been hotter that time because not only did we wear the glasses for our trip, but Jan had no jersey under her sunsuit nor did I under my strap-held plaid-trimmed pedal pushers. Those outfits must have been stock ones for the shore because we wore them in photographs both times.

Neighbors told mother they didn't know how she did it, getting all of us packed every Sunday. They admired her. They said they couldn't do it. The Connecticut Transit Bus Company pickup location was near the corner of Gold and Main Street in downtown Hartford. We waited on the Gold Street side of the Palace Theater, which had its entrance on Main Street. We first walked up Hungerford north, right onto Russ, crossed Buckingham, and down Capital past the Bushnell Memorial Theater to Clinton Street across Elm and through the park to Gold. The walk took twenty minutes, give or take a minute or two. No matter how early we arrived, there were always people there before us. They stood in groups with the same paraphernalia we had, unloaded onto the sidewalk and waiting until the buses came.

And come they did, the blue transit buses, turning the corner onto Gold from Elm Street at ten o'clock. The flurry of the hustle and bustle that coincided with the first vehicles scared my sister and me. The buses headed for several beaches including Hammonasset but also Sound View, Rocky Neck, and Ocean Beach. There was a run on each bus—no, a stampede—and it was then we felt our fellow travelers as they rushed, shoved, bumped, and stepped on feet as they elbowed their way to the bus entrance. Jan whimpered, and I didn't blame her. No one, it seemed, had manners when it came to grabbing a seat for family and friends. But Mom told me, "Grandma was one of the worst. She pushed and shoved with the rest of them and looked mad whenever anyone interrupted her rush to grab two seats for us." Mom and Dad occupied one and Grandma, Jan, and I, a second. And I thought of the people who had to drive their cars to the beach and missed all this excitement.

The bus journey became fun after we sat down and got going. The cost was a dollar or two. The driver collected the fare on the bus. Mom said, "It couldn't have cost more because we couldn't have afforded to go." Small beach bags and umbrellas were put up on a rack, and the larger parcels lined the narrow aisle between the two long rows of bus seats.

The trip from Hartford to Hammonasset in Madison took about an hour and a half. People chatted, but Jan and I looked out of the windows at buildings and scenery rarely seen except on those Sunday excursions. The bus took back roads. We drove through Hartford, Wethersfield, Rocky Hill, Cromwell, Middletown, Durham, and finally to Madison. I saw the first of Hammonasset Beach, a Connecticut State Park, on a stretch of road just before we turned right to the entrance. Through some bushes and trees—there it was. Our resort. The sky met the water, and no buildings marred the view.

Drivers of the five buses parked them in a West Beach dirt lot, one of two sections of Hammonasset, and about a five-minute walk to the bath houses in the Grand Pavilion. You had to remember the bus number you came on and where the driver parked. Those vehicles remained there, neatly parked side by side, as if patiently waiting for us to have our day away from the hot city.

The next rush after we got out of the bus was to grab a table in the pavilion for lunch. Grandma was the aggressive one again, and when she found the ideal table, one nearest the boardwalk with an unobstructed view of the water, she plunked the wooden lunch basket down like the table belonged to her. And it did—for the day. This was all a prelude for Jan and me. The reason to come was for sand and water, and we couldn't wait for the grown-up business of food, tables, and settling in, to finish.

Grandma and Mom wearing the locker keys.

We could change in the aging wooden bathhouses free, but to secure our clothes and not have to lug them on the beach with the towels, shovels, pails, boats, and umbrella, you could, for a small fee, get a key to lock them up for the day. And whereas my family couldn't afford frills, we could this one. There were separate entrances for men and women. Mom put Dad's things in with ours, so we needed one locker. Photographs show Grandma and Mom wearing the white cord necklace which held the long key on the end of it. The key's number matched the locker number. Jan and I had fun finding the match.

The bathhouses, Clam Shed, concession area, huge picnic decks, boardwalks, and ramps all built in 1929 of the same wood that had grayed by 1949 and the early 1950s. Wooden railings flanked the ramps, and the boardwalks built high off the sand provided play areas and some relief from the heat. But Mom, who loved the sun and us in it, didn't tolerate that long. "I didn't bring you kids to the beach to play in the shade. Come out of there." But the boardwalk made itself felt as the day lengthened. Its wood blistered our feet, and we took some of it home as slivers.

We sometimes met a couple of aunts and half a dozen cousins there. The day was coordinated beforehand, and we shared a plot of beach and lunch table. The constant sun gave no relief, even under a beach umbrella that didn't always create enough shade for everyone when relatives joined us. But there was the great ocean of Long Island Sound to cool us. To get in over the scorching sand, like a gauntlet, often required using the corners of other sunbathers' towels to relieve, if for an instant, the torture of getting to the ocean.

Sometimes relatives joined us.

Breezes sent the green-gray water of the Sound with cresting caps of white foam, to greet us. The surf slapped the shore and water met the sand, enticing us in. Too young for swim lessons in the 1940's, Jan and I only jumped around in the water wearing our yellow one-piece bathing suits that had no top or played ring-around-the-rosy with Grandma who loved bobbing up and down holding our hands as we slowly circled and sang to the Mother Goose song to the rhythm of the waves: "Ring around the rosy, a pocket full of posies; ashes, ashes, all fall down!" Like her dress, Grandma's skirted bathing suit was flowered. She replaced her black oxfords with sneakers for the water. But then, because she wore sneaks, she never felt the ache of those small rocks and pebbles assaulting our feet like another gauntlet, this time in the ocean.

Jan and I launched our boats and as they bobbed up and down on the waves, hovered over them like conscientious captains making sure they didn't float out to sea.

There were not many of those Sundays when Daddy didn't get his fair-freckled skin sunburned or get called in by the lifeguard who blew a whistle because Daddy swam beyond the marker. Dad swam well. Mom did a decent dog paddle. Spaced along the beach, the lifeguards sat in tall chairs of wood with three wrap-around boards they used to climb to their seat. And each sat there above us in hats shielding them from the relentless sun.

At four thirty, we gathered up our belongings, washed our things of the salt water, and headed for the bathhouses which had been built under the concession and picnic areas of the pavilion and formed the second level. Shafts of light squeezed through the slabs of the wood walls, giving some light to an otherwise dark lower interior. There, pulling on a long chain, we showered in cold water. Grandma always held Jan and me under to make sure all of the sand and salt water got left at Hammonasset. The sand washed off us and fell between the glistening cracks of the wet wood, returning to the beach under the houses. Our claw-foot tub at our Hartford flat offered only baths so, cold as it was, a shower was a treat. There was no dawdle time. The buses left at five. Not a minute before or after.

"You kids always fell asleep on the way home," Mom said. "You looked so fresh after the shower, so tanned. I used to wake you when we got to Rocky Hill for ice cream."

The stop on the way home for a cone featured another highlight that came with the bus trip. In the fifties, 3272 Main Street, Rocky Hill, was an ice cream establishment, The Fountain. We got out, stretched our legs, and ordered ice creams to refresh us. My favorite was pistachio with nuts. We walked around the parking lot for a while, licking the ice cream from the cones. From there it took twenty minutes before we reached Hartford.

The bus driver dropped us off where we began on Gold Street, and we reversed everything done in the morning. At the front door, we said tired goodbyes to Grandma and went upstairs. We hoped for a sunny Sunday next week.

The Cohens

S ometimes we get to know people by watching them. But then we have only the outline of their lives. I wish it weren't the case that little attention paid to some people results in missed friendships that might have developed had one done more than just watch.

I got to know a Mr. and Mrs. Cohen by observing them from my back porch. They were my neighbors in the 1940s and 1950s when I was growing up in the Frog Hollow in Hartford. They lived in, and probably owned, the three-family 1897 Hungerford Street brick tenement next door numbered 123–125. Our tenement at 119–121, built in the same year and designed by the same architect, looked structurally like theirs down to the iron handrailings that flanked the wooden front steps of each building. But, although identical architecturally, the buildings were fraternally dressed. The second and third-floor front porches on the Cohens' building were gone from ours. They maintained and protected the wood on their porches with a dark brown paint also used on the banisters, doors, floors, and window trim in front and back. Our trim, Grandma had painted dark red and white. It was like the Cohens didn't want to draw attention to themselves with bright colors.

The couple could have been in their sixties or seventies. A short, stocky pair, each had gray hair, though most of Mr. Cohen's had deserted his head and what nature had left of Mrs. Cohen's, she controlled in tight curls. Each wore wire spectacles, and whether shopping or going to the beach, they dressed up. She wore variations of a multicolored flower print dress and beige cotton stockings, which ended in a pair of thick-heeled black laced shoes. Her outfits looked similar to my grandmother's. I'd say the only frivolity Mrs. Cohen allowed herself were flowers—those on her dresses and those on a certain tree. Mr. Cohen wore a white shirt and black trousers often enough to call it a uniform, and he looked hot in summer. The black jacket that went with them, he kept on unless the temperature hit a hundred or more.

What further defined Mr. and Mrs. Cohen? They were Jewish—Jewish on a street of Christians—and so as foreign to me as some of our immigrant Polish and Lithuanian neighbors. I didn't know then what it meant to be Jewish but often wondered whether because they were Jews, they avoided me or I them.

There were other differences distinguishing the Cohens. And one stood in their front yard—a white magnolia tree that bloomed early every spring, showing off its white outfit, a striking contrast to the dull-looking building it stood in front of and the simple tastes of the couple. Spiffed up in our new Easter clothes, the magnolia provided a perfect background for our pictures. But was anything on Easter Sunday so adorned as Mr. and Mrs. Cohen's tree with its soft, white perennial petals? Not me.

A silver chain-link fence penned the tree in. Short bushes lined the fence on the yard side, companions highlighting the tree's beauty. That magnolia was the gilded lily of Hungerford Street, strewing its petals generously on the Cohens' otherwise unadorned front stone slab sidewalk. Whether or not the couple themselves planted the tree or inherited it when they moved in, I couldn't tell you. But I do know the blossoms could be seen from one end of Hungerford at Park to the other at Capitol Avenue—if you stood in the middle of the street.

Even a local newspaper, *The Hartford Courant*, photographed the tree. We were all proud, especially my mother. "Look, the Cohens' tree got in the paper. Isn't that nice? Makes our street look good."

In fact, if ever anyone asked directions to the Cohen address around springtime, you might answer, "Look for the house with the beautiful white magnolia tree in front. You can't miss it." As far as I know, no one had ever asked about, let alone visited the couple.

Mr. and Mrs. Cohen probably didn't, as we said, "come from money," but seemed rich because they owned an automobile. Few on Hungerford Street did in those early years, so they were more modern than many of us who still walked or took the bus to go anywhere. My family never owned a car until I got mine in 1960 when I graduated high school. The Cohens' small, black Ford looked antique in the 1950s. Like them, it was small, neat, and compact. Mr. Cohen drove and used the car for two reasons I know of—to shop or go to the beach. My family took a bus from Gold Street in downtown Hartford to Hammonasset Beach, lugging everything we needed for the day. Mr. and Mrs. Cohen went many sunny Sundays, and looked like anything but beach people, dressed up as they always were. I asked my mother if she thought they ever changed into bathing suits at the shore. "They must get wet because Mrs. Cohen hangs two towels on the line after she returns," she said.

The garage for their Ford took over space that might have been used for a backyard, hogging at least three quarters of the lot. But why would the Cohens need a yard as big as ours anyway as they never lounged or dallied outside? The garage was old even when I was a kid. Built of clapboards, it had a flat black tar paper roof that accumulated water that stubbornly sat on it after every rain until the summer sun coaxed it dry. And, as if cooperating with the Cohens' color scheme, nature had aged the clapboards to a dark brown that couldn't have matched the house better had the couple painted them. The garage showed up in the background of many of our backyard snapshots. The garage floor was dirt and the windows, that miserly let light into it, were grimy and dark, reinforced with wire to discourage break-ins.

The garage entrance, at the front right, Mr. Cohen opened using one of two big iron handles on each of two oversized doors. One door first and then the other sliding on noisy rollers, both cumbersome, rumbling and rocking on their metal slides as they were pulled left, loud as an empty tender traveling railroad tracks. I have yet to see a set of garage doors like them.

Besides the Cohens' car that took up little space in the huge garage, two or three other drivers, who might have been the first and second-floor renters in the tenement, shared the space. And, although "A Garage for Rent" sign was nailed to the right-hand side front porch pillar, there were never more than those few cars in the garage at one time. So the Cohens, who left it three quarters empty, didn't seem to need the money. Mother said they were retired before they moved to Hungerford Street.

The garage shared the yard with an open wooden shed housing three galvanized garbage pails piled over their rims especially on holidays. The lids, perched on top and waiting to fall off, provided easy access to the leftover delectables for rats that ran boldly about in everyone's open shed back then. Scrappy forsythia bushes provided a backdrop for the shed and the rest of the yard east side of us. Several large blocks of stone slabs plopped along from the back porch steps to the garage shed made do for a walking path. The chain-link fence in back was an extension of the front one. The only green growing in the yard besides the few forsythia were wisps of grass. The magnolia in front seemed enough landscaping.

But what also set the Cohens apart besides their being Jewish and the magnolia tree, was a big pulley rigged up to serve them. The pulley, suspended from their third-floor back porch, the side facing us, was one of a kind not only on our street but in the entire Frog Hollow. I'd bet in all of Hartford.

Most Hungerford Street back porches were open, but the Cohens had theirs boarded up on the sides, vertical laths providing privacy, maybe protection, from the first to their third floor. The pulley, a conspicuous ingenious piece of machinery, hung there, a reminder of good ole Yankee ingenuity whether built by a Yankee or not. It was a long fixture with a handle that turned a wheel when a drop flap was released under it. Inside, a thick coiled rope was attached to a big silver hook.

Downstairs, in a precoordinated ritual born of routine, Mr. Cohen took either shopping or beach paraphernalia out of the trunk, put it on the ground near double cellar doors in a spot under the pulley. Mrs. Cohen arranged the parts and parcels while he rolled the garage doors shut on the Ford. She waited for him to reach the third floor and unlatch the small wooden door cut out of their porch side to reach the pulley. After he had unhooked the bottom of the pulley, he looked down and said, "All right, send them up," and turned the handle to lower the hook to the waiting Mrs. Cohen. She put as many of her handled bags on the hook as he could comfortably bring up. Mr. Cohen turned the handle slowly, and the bags swayed back and forth on their shortcut ride to the third floor. Trying not to seem nosy, I pretended not to watch from my second-floor back-porch sitting in a chair in the sun. I sometimes got caught watching their unique ritual. "Hello," Mrs. Cohen would say. "Nice day."

"Hello, Mrs. Cohen. Yes, it is." No conversation with her or her husband was ever longer.

Those were times when life offered nothing more exciting than a couple returning from the beach on a late Sunday afternoon. I can still hear the sound of the old Ford as Mr. Cohen drove it slowly, carefully along the narrow alley between our tenement and theirs, to the backyard, car wheels crunching the loose stone and dirt, then opening and closing the huge garage doors, and the up-and-down cranking of that pulley.

One day those two old neighbors weren't there anymore. When they left, I never noticed. And now they reside in memory, their property in the background of old slides and photographs.

I wish, though, I had told them just once, "I like your pulley."

Pope Park

In the 1950s, when I was a child, there stood the half-century-old Pope Park. It looked swell for its age. No kid or adult I ever saw abused it, and city fathers maintained it during the years when my family, friends, and I used it. No one feared going to Pope Park; no one was scared in it.

The park's birth year was 1895. That was when Hartford's premier industrialist, Colonel Albert A. Pope, gave land to Hartford's residents for recreation and to "promote lives of health, happiness, and order." In his honor, city fathers named the park Pope.

Let me tell you what Pope Park was once upon a time, and why I loved it.

One mile from the scorching summer sidewalks, roads, and tenements of Hungerford Street in the Frog Hollow section of Hartford, there was a getaway, a relief from the fried inner city, an urban oasis—Pope Park. In the first half of the 1950s, during my summer release from Dominick F. Burns Grammar School, I walked to Pope to escape a hot second-floor flat in a three-story brick tenement, which got built before air-conditioning or central air. Pope Park became my "Florida" where the sun followed but got neutralized by the sparking blue, cold chlorine water of the park's pool—an "ocean" in cement dug out of the landscape of the park's seventy-five acres.

That manicured landscape offered not only the pool but a playground of swings, slides, monkey bars, and seesaws. But it was to the park's swimming pool that I made the trek to Pope, the pool's water a salve for the sunburns and blisters the sun plastered me with in July and August. It was to the pool I walked the mile to cool off, have fun, get free swim lessons, and later compete on the swim team.

There were lots of routes to and from the park from Hungerford—a myriad of sunbaked streets to go up or down. Mostly I used two—the Russ Street route up and Park Street back. In the earlier years, Mom walked me there. When I got older, I went by myself.

Out of 119 Hungerford, a left took me north about three minutes and then another left onto Russ past a dozen three-story brick tenements like ours, except the Russ Street ones had more of the second and third-floor front porches I liked. An Armenian drugstore where my family bought papers and other things anchored the block on the south side. The brick Volodimir Ukrainian Orthodox Church across the street on Russ's north side held the other end. We walked across Broad toward Lawrence Street by the Billings Forge factory, its machines droning through windows open to capture a breeze to fan its roasting interior. I felt sorry for the workers in Billings because no matter how hot I might have been on the way to the pool, they were hotter. The Forge took up the entire north side block between Babcock and Putnam Streets. D. F. Burns occupied the corner and hill from Putnam to Park Terrace.

The Baby Park and tennis courts.

From the Terrace, I hadn't much farther to go but first passed the small Baby Park in Pope North, a park prelude. It had a few play-things, benches, and red clay tennis courts. A High Line fence kept our tennis balls off the streets.

And finally, there it was—Pope Park South—stretched out across Park Street, showing off much of its acres of lawn, trees, and flowers, all a wonderful natural expanse where I could, for a few hours, desert Hartford's heat.

The south section of the park had on it a pool for fish and frogs and was bordered by weeds and willows. Near the pond, a small wooden shelter had been built for ice-skaters in winter. On the west side of Pope near the corner of Park Terrace and Park stood the Pope Park bathhouse. The building hugged the street, and the surround-ing trees, their branches spread out like so many umbrellas, sheltered it from the persistent summer sun. Entrance signs indicated one for men and one for women. The bathhouse personnel discouraged kids. My mother said vagrant men used the place and she warned me, "If you don't need to go in there, don't." A woman in a starched white uniform gave out a small square of soap and a towel for a fee. She kept the place spotless and scowled when kids needed to use the lavatories before or after a day at Pope.

At Pope Park Drive, straight ahead on a hill, a chain-link fence that corralled the pool, a gray wooden bathhouse, and attached brown concession stand showed themselves. Benches and playground stood to the right and behind them, a dark overgrown marsh area had been created and kept wet by the Hog River. It was said quicksand bubbled somewhere in there. No sign warned me away but the area was unofficially off-limits. I crossed over to Park South across Pope Park Drive, the quickest way to the pool.

Those were good times trudging to the park, suit rolled in a towel, to my resort in the city, thanks to Mr. Pope. And we came from all directions, an unsynchronized march of kids in skimpy tops and short shorts, most of us wearing our bathing suit to save time jumping into the pool. I carried all I needed to make a day at the park perfect: swimsuit, bathing cap, towel, and comb.

And the park served me well. Swimming lessons began when I was eight. My younger sister would have hers some years later. Mother walked my sister and me to the park every day during our summer vacations so, as she said, "You kids could learn to swim." She not only patiently walked us up to Pope day after day but stood outside the link fence and watched us struggle lesson after lesson. Nothing but words of encouragement from her, deserved or not. "Good, that was good," she'd say and nod her head and smile. I feared taking both feet off the pool floor and was terrified the first time I had to float away from my lifeline—the pool's edge. I'd later earn a Red Cross certificate, and a few years later, join the swim team. Mom was proud.

We sat on the lawn near the concession stand after the lessons, and she unpacked our lunch. At the concession stand attached to the bathhouse, I'd eat my pretzels bought for a penny a stick after the pool and lesson. I got five. Lugging the chlorine smell in a rolled up towel dampened by suit and bathing cap, pretzels in hand, I headed for the playground, and Mom sat on a bench to wait. Of all the playthings offered, I liked the swings best. I dropped the towel on what little grass was left near them and pushed off the dry dirt that sent up tiny dust puffs. I swung up and down like a pendulum, lulled after the walk and swim. The steel slides stood in front and were often too hot to use being in the sun all day. The monkey bars and craft area with its benches stood right of the slides. On a swing, under a blue sky and trees planted generously around the playground like umbrellas to shade the sun, life couldn't be more perfect. Once in a rambunctious while, I jumped off when the swing's wooden seat, held by thick iron links, peaked before coming down. In the very early days when learning to swim, Mom would be part of these rituals until I was older and able to go alone with my Hungerford Street friends.

The swim instructors were brothers who worked as lifeguards too. Phil, Jimmy, and Ronnie Evans were handsome, and I had a crush on all three. Blond, blue-eyed, and tan, they strolled the cement boardwalk around the pool from the shallow to the deep end as if the pool belonged to them. They were relaxed, swinging a whistle on a long cord, twirling and untwirling it around a finger, strolling around watching our aquatic shows often put on for them. We, kids, who passed the brothers' tough swim program, showed off our strokes. You could see passing grades for the crawl, back or side stroke, but not many, including me, had mastered the butterfly or breaststrokes. And the two diving boards thumped as our dives and cannonballs threw the blue water up into the hot air where it rained back down on us. But mostly the brothers kept an eye out for each of us splashing, swimming, and laughing as we cooled ourselves off in those summers that seemed endless.

Later and older, I went to the pool myself. There were two afternoon shifts. I tried to get the earlier one, but come late and you waited until one Evans brother blew his whistle to end the first so the second shift could start. And the line we waited in outside was long, and the time to get inside seemed forever. But there was the pool to empty of kids reluctant to get out, wet suits to peel off, redressing, and grooming before the bathhouse emptied. And we, in shift two, stood side by side, pressed up against the pool's wire fence, as my mother had for years, rolled towels trapped under an arm, like somber still lives, envying the kids in shift one, soaking, cooling off, and screeching arias of pleasure. Like partners in patience, we waited, fingers clutching the fence for a time longer than eternity as the shift dragged to an end.

There was a hitch, though, to getting in and that was height. Measure one fraction below the forty-two inches and you were, as the attendant said, "Outta luck, kid. Maybe next time." You came back another month, another summer. It was funny but sad to see little kids who, pulled aside to get measured, stretch themselves as much as they could without standing on their toes to make the mark.

Before being allowed into the pool, rules required a shower soak. The freezing water that tumbled out of Pope Park's shower nozzles, competed with the ones at Hammonasset—the water was ice-cold in both places. Shivering before sweating, I sat at the diving board end of the pool, my back up against the bathhouse clapboards, fanny on the cement to warm up, and checked out who was who in the water. I hoped all the Evans brothers showed up. Finally in the pool and sucking a sigh at the cold, I dolphin dived from the shallow end until the water got too deep. Before a swim to the deep end, I checked the lane. But no matter how much surveillance, there was always some kid who jumped or swam smack in front of me, ruining a stroke, or almost drowning me. Most boys hopped out of the pool ignoring the ladders. I once tried hopping out. After that try, I continued using the ladder.

If I walked Russ Street to the pool, I used the Park Street route home. Between Park Terrace and Putnam on Park stood a string of tenements built on a hill. My mother knew some girl who lived there, and every time we happened in the area, even years later, she never failed to say, "I used to know a girl who lived in one of those buildings, but I don't remember which one." Jane Hart located her dance school on the corner of Park and Park Terrace on the south side. I can still hear my friend, Carol, who thumped away in patent leather tap shoes on the wooden floor at Hart's studio with no hope of ever becoming a Ginger Rogers. I walked the north side of Park. On the next block, Babcock, was St. Anne's or the "French" church as we called it. Roth's Men's Clothier shared the same area. I could see myself in Roth's big picture windows, which took up most of the storefront. Roth's stood on the block between Babcock and Laurence. The ice shop was there, too, on the south side. The lemon ice cup held just enough of the treat, which I ate first and slurped after as it melted. For five cents, I got crushed lemon ice in a soft-fluted paper cup. Before our childhood ended, we must have made the shopkeeper a millionaire with our nickels.

The block to Broad Street included Dr. Eliot's office on one side and Kofsky's shoe store on the other. But the block between Broad and Hungerford was the commercial center of our lives—our block. There was the Immaculate Conception Church I attended with my grandmother, mother, and sister and which got so crowded some Sundays, parishioners were shepherded to the basement to hear mass; Woolworth's and the five-and-ten cent store, where my family bought everything; the Lyric Theater Joe ran across the street and where I sat every Saturday morning for the kiddie show; and next to it, Aunt Millie's store, where my mother worked with her sister in the early 50s. Nearby was the Lincoln Dairy, which sold the best and biggest ice cream cones. All stood facing each other on Park's north or south side together with a delicatessen on the corner of Broad and Park where we bought bagels and the *Courant* every Sunday morning after mass. Across the street stood a shop that sold knickknacks. One, an Asian figure squatting in front of a big bowl, I bought for my mother on Mother's Day. I still have it. These blocks on Park Street, combined commercial and residential, created a street teeming with people all day.

I made my way home from Pope Park on streets that connected me to buildings and the people who lived and worked in them—a neighborhood where I played out a routine year after year—from the start to the end of summer vacation trudging up to that urban park with its pool and playground to participate in a rite of childhood that fortified me physically, mentally, socially, and competitively. Pope Park is 124 years old now, but I think it lost its youth a long time ago. I think it lost its youth the day I made my walk up and back for the last time.

The Clothesline

By the 1950s, my mother owned a Frederick Louis Maytag washing machine. But drying laundry wasn't as modern for Mom as the washing of it. For that she still used a clothes-line. In fact, given the laundry-blocked view from our second-floor tenement back porch on a Monday morning at 119 Hungerford Street in Hartford's Frog Hollow, every neighbor dried laundry on a clothesline.

The line, a sturdy but thin rope attached to a pole set in at the back end of the property and strung out from there to our porch, looped through aluminum wheels at each end. The rope itself looked like it could be used for double Dutch–for giants. By the midfifties, the pole, worn thin by time and weather, was held up by two pieces of tall lumber shoved against it for support.

The line's knotted excess rope hung down like an appendage. The aluminum pulley, sent out in the middle of a day's laundry, held the line taut and balanced so as not to sag and tangle up with Grandma's wash hanging on the first floor.

On a nail under the back porch clothesline wheel hung a cloth clothespin bag that the elements had faded. The bag held a collection of wooden clothespins people sometimes made into ornaments given their round head and two legs. Later, Mom mixed those clothespins with updated ones that a spring opened when one squeezed the two notched legs together. The new pin's serrated grip secured the clothes. But in a wind, clothespins dropped to the lawn. Before my father mowed, my sister and I had to pick them up. Those missed got noisily chewed up by the mower and Grandma complained, "Why didn't you kids pick up the clothes pins? I can't afford to sharpen the blades all the time."

A chore before Mom hung the clothes out was to clean the line with a damp cloth to rid it of dirt and bird droppings left after the last wash. Birds and bugs used the clothesline as their personal high wire.

My mother perfected hanging out wash. I asked her once, "Why do you always do the same thing? Why so fussy about hanging out the clothes in a certain order?" She told me about Mrs. Cherwinski, who lived two tenements down from us and also lived on the second floor.

"I used to watch her hang wash out. I admired the way she put like items in order on her line. And she hung everything just so. I wanted my clothesline to look neat like hers."

When the sun shone, especially on a crisp day, Mom brought the clothes in an armful at a time, her face buried in the fresh wash. She'd hold them out to me. "Smell these. There's nothing more wonderful than clothes with fresh air in them."

"They do smell nice," I replied, because they did.

In winter when she brought in clothes, including Dad's very often stiff trousers, she stood them up in the kitchen. Thawing out near our Florence stove, they became limp, buckled, and collapsed in a heap. Clothes that didn't dry Mom draped over furniture or decorated the bathroom with them until dry.

Our clothes, bedding, and bath items, displayed on that line season after season, flapped, bobbed, and waved like performers on a tightrope, drying in the summer heat or winter cold. Blown high in a wind, some clothes strained to fly. Empty shirtsleeves hanging and swaying loosely upside down looked like kids swinging on park monkey bars. Trousers pinned at the waist, with pockets turned out, resembled suspects a cop frisked. Sheets like flattened Halloween ghosts created anemic backgrounds captured in photographs.

Wind and sun dried most clothes in my neighborhood in the forties and fifties when I was young. Today a dryer does the work. The fresh air which clung to my mother's wash is now in a box of Bounce which promises in English, French, and Spanish your clothes will be "fresh air fresh."

Without me in them, my clothes would no longer get outside. Crunched, they go round and round in a dryer after washing, get pulled out and dumped into a basket when done, and lugged up from a basement. They never see the light of day anymore to fresh air-dry.

Housewives like Mom and Mrs. Cherwinski, hanging wash out, socializing across clotheslines as they dipped into the clothespin bag and wheeled laundry out, exist now in memory or in the background of Brownie black-and-white snapshots.

The Bath

Don't get me wrong. I adored my grandmother. I loved her. But she was responsible for the primitive way my family and I took baths throughout my younger years in the 1940s and 1950s in our second-floor bathroom on Hungerford Street. It wasn't any old flat but a cold-water one. I guess someone could argue that Grandma, by not installing hot water for us, gird us for hardships later and gave us a grit of spirit not everyone could lay claim to—certainly not my neighbors who lived with the luxury of hot water.

I took a bath once a week on Saturday evening. One luxury all of us shared in our late 1890s flat, was the claw–footed tub. Today only the wealthy afford one, but back then they were beautiful and standard fixtures along with ivory hot and cold faucet tops. To enhance and complement the tub, Mom fixed the bathroom cute. The door stayed open when not in use. Not only was the outer bathtub painted blue, but most other things in the room were, including a small piece of furniture, the hamper top, the wallboard, and a shelf. Pretty decorations finished the room.

For my bath, Mom filled two huge pails with water to set on the stove's gas burners to heat. It took twenty or so minutes to get hot. Then one of us carried the pails into the bathroom, made sure the plug was in, and poured the hot water from each pail into the tub. Cold water was added. I tested the temperature by running my hand back and forth, back and forth in the water to get it just right. Assured I wouldn't scald or freeze, I got in. The shallow water itself just about covered my legs and no more. I couldn't dawdle as my sister would bathe next in the same water. The routine continued for many years. In-between bathing was done by what we called a sponge bath.

And if you ask me if anything could get more primitive regarding bathing, I'd say yes. I recalled the set tub in the kitchen. It was a huge stone tub with a metal cover that one raised to wash children and clothing in. The set tub had two openings, a left-hand side that had faucets but no cover and was smaller. Grandma had the set tub removed, but I liked it. Jan and I had been washed in it a few times.

The direct hand I had in making things function is my memoir's nostalgic heart and includes the benefit of not having had it easy.

The Veranda

The picture of a veranda and the scenes of summer played on it remain pasted in memory. The veranda would remain unchanged for me no matter what became of it in the years between childhood and adulthood.

Located across the street from my grandmother's three-story tenement where I lived on 119 Hungerford Street, the veranda at 118 was the first thing I saw every day when I left the house. It was one of a kind. If asked how many houses had verandas on Hungerford Street in the Frog Hollow section of Hartford where I grew up in the forties and fifties, I'd say, "Only a few." Instead, most buildings had a small porch to get to the first-floor entrance, usually the landlord's place, or the second- and third-floor entrances where tenants lived.

Unlike a veranda, a porch, built open and small, didn't offer shelter against sun and rain, and if you wanted to sit, the stairs would have to do. Most of the three-family brick tenement houses on the street, built around the late 1890s, had a porch but no veranda. But at 118 Hungerford, at Bill and Ann's, it was different.

"I wish Grandma's house had a big veranda like Bill and Ann's," my mother used to say. "It would be so nice. You could at least put chairs on it, have neighbors over." Back then when we said veranda, we meant bigger than a porch. And the wooden extension, the veranda at 118, measured twice the size of our porch. In 1896, when 118 Hungerford was built, designers cared about how places looked even for the immigrants pouring in from Europe to work the typewriter factories and small shops. They all seemed to land on Hungerford Street to live—the Italians, Irish, Greeks, Poles, Lithuanians, and Armenians. I think they came to Frog Hollow for more than just the work though. I bet word had spread in Europe what a fine neighborhood we had. The veranda helped us get acquainted with people and make friends.

Bill and Ann's veranda, built high off the street, needed not only seven wooden steps but two cement ones with an extra landing of sidewalk to get to the veranda's floor. If you felt like climbing the two sets of steps, their veranda became a place to gather and socialize. It was worth the climb. "Sitting here, I can see the street north to Capitol Avenue, south to Park Street, and every neighbor who passes, Bill tried making us believe. Most houses, a driveway apart, had front sidewalks, making it easy to get from house to house.

Ann and Bill never had their stairs and porch floor painted anything but a battleship gray, and every time they did, my mother said, "Too bad they don't use a darker paint. It would look better with the hunter-green trim."

But light or dark deck paint, nothing took away from the beauty and elegance of that veranda which extended not only along the two front entrances but wrapped itself, in gallery style, around the three bay windows that overlooked it. The added wraparound space let Bill and Ann set chairs out, including a rocker, making it a treat for neighbors to stop and pass time getting and giving gossip. People must have lived less hectic lives back then because some neighbor was always sitting up there in the summertime.

And if the veranda wasn't unique and beautiful enough, to gild the lily, there was the awning. Every summer Bill got together the hardware that held and extended the only one on the street. Someone always remarked, "There goes Bill with the awning. Summer's here." The awning of dark-green-and-gray canvas stripe with a frill along its edge spread over the veranda like a pretty but heavy parasol to keep us cool in its shadow. Air-conditioning spoiled few of us in the forties and fifties, so for Bill's family, escaping the heat of summer meant getting to the veranda, a cool extension of the hot inside.

The veranda built in Colonial Revival style looked southern with its eight sturdy, smooth Doric columns. Those columns held up a pediment, a triangular decoration that crowned the roof, all painted hunter green. Inside the pediment, on a part architects call the tympanum, a half sun, with radiating beams like arms welcoming guests, had been carved. Standard then, the decorations today would cost a fortune. We didn't always visit across the street to just sit and talk however, we also drank in my later years.

The veranda became a summer bar, and I shared the toasts. "How about a drink today, Lynn," Bill or Ann asked. If ever I refused, I can't recall.

And when asked, "The usual?"

I said, "Yes," and got a Southern Comfort with cranberry juice served in a glass cooled and clinking with ice.

The veranda helped forge friendships which lasted a lifetime. That wonderful hodgepodge of people in Hartford in the Frog Hollow section on Hungerford Street I socialized so often with on the veranda are gone now. Most left for the suburbs in the late fifties and sixties when factories, manufacturing centers, and shops closed. They took with them a way of life and a neighborhood. Frog Hollow and Hungerford Street would struggle forever to recover.

But years later, I wondered what happened to that veranda, wondered if anything from my Hungerford Street time remained.

One early morning, I pulled onto Hungerford from Capitol Avenue and crossed Russ Street to my old neighborhood. Current landlords beautifully converted some of the houses to law offices, leaving them stunning but empty looking. Many were used only from 9:00 a.m. to 5:00 p.m. No one remained in the evening hours.

A few verandas had been reduced to porches and porches to landings. I drove slowly past eight houses.

If to recognize the veranda required my stopping, then I'd have driven by. For in that early hour with just enough light, I saw a wreck.

The wooden steps, each gouged, would no longer support anyone. One of the two handrailings along the stairs was gone including the balustrade around the veranda itself. The balustrade had fallen neatly propped up against what remained of the wooden tongue-and-groove skirt below. The missing part of skirt around the base offered a look under the veranda not possible before. The gray-and-green paint, faded and peeling, looked like blisters on old, dry skin. Now, each split down the middle, the five remaining columns no longer supported the roof alone but got help, like crutches supporting an invalid, from two huge pieces of lumber sloppily shoved against the roof. Round circles, like scars on rotting wood, marked the places of missing columns. A half-tied long piece of dirty plastic yellow-and-black tape tied to a front column warned of danger. Stout plywood boards muffled the bay windows and front entrances. And only the snout of a drain pipe remained around the edge of the roof.

Two people walking by turned and looked back, wondering I'm sure, what it was about a decaying veranda and abandoned building that held anyone's interest.

But despite everything, promises of hope presented themselves that early morning. The pediment over the veranda floor had remained intact, too high for people to ruin. Time had spared it too. Its half sun still radiated beams like outstretched arms of a host waiting to greet guests again. And the yellow piece of plastic tied around the column—a symbol of support and hope for restoration. A big blue-and-yellow notice from the Hartford Housing Authority, slapped onto one of the window's plywood boards, was a sign someone knew the veranda and the house it clung to were still there.

It took years before 118 Hungerford with the veranda was restored and looked identical to the memory I had of it those decades ago when I sat on it with friends in the lazy days of summer.

119 Hungerford Street

My world was Hartford's Frog Hollow and a building on Hungerford Street—the theater with its setting and stages wherein I played out my childhood.

I take you to this building, into it, around it, to see what it meant and still means to me, because it provided the home wherein I spent the first forty-six years of my life. The Hungerford Street building in the Hollow was forty-five years old when I was born. It would celebrate its ninety-first birthday when I moved out, having hosted my childhood and adulthood. I would not spend old age there. Until 1988, 119 Hungerford was the only home I knew. I carry fond memories of it with me now in my senior years.

Similar in structure to buildings found throughout the Frog Hollow section of Hartford, our three-family tenement of red brick, brownstone, and wood trim was built in 1897 on Hungerford Street's west side. The brownstone, which rimmed its base, workers quarried in Portland, Connecticut. My grandmother owned our home. Architects called it a half-six, characterized by three stories with bowed front windows. Like many of its kind in the Frog Hollow, 119 Hungerford provided a residence for three families, most of whose heads of households worked in one of many industrial businesses in the area. Two included typewriter firms, the Underwood and the Royal, both providing most jobs. Industrial activity along Capitol Avenue and other Hartford Streets stimulated residential development when many owners sold their farmland for housing lots. The new tenements would accommodate the flood of workers to the Frog Hollow. But 119 Hungerford was much more than a structure, more than its brick, mortar, and wood. My childhood and adulthood home encapsulated fond remembrances of my family and provided a backdrop where familial bonds were forged. The strength and love within the building girded me in transition from child to adult.

The front porch entrance to 119 provided only a platform, like a small wooden stage, where Grandmother accessed the left side door to her first-floor flat, and we, the right-hand one that led to the second floor. Renters lived on the third floor. Ours wasn't a full veranda like the one Ann and Bill had across the street. At best, you could set a chair down or sit on the steps as I often did.

Grandma had this entrance porch floor and steps painted mostly dark battleship gray, the balustrades and pillars cream. The porch's pitched roof was plain and covered with black shingles. My mother said the building once boasted second and third story front porches, like balconies overlooking the streetscape scenery. They rotted so had been removed long before I was born.

To the left of the porch door, to the second- and third-floor flats, hung our metal mailboxes with flip lids and slots to see the mail. The 1940s and 1950s were years when correspondence was done by mail, and mailmen walked their street beats to get it to us.

The boxes shared some of the space with a bell buzzer shell that rang out its permission to come in when pushed upstairs in our kitchen, allowing the door to open. Outdated and not working consistently when I was young, the voice response shell that let us speak to the person waiting on the porch, was even then anachronistic. I wish, like the upper front porches, this feature had lasted to accompany me through childhood. I missed the potential fun of having these unique features to use.

The front porch paneled door with its white lace curtain opened onto the downstairs small front hall. The wooden staircase to the second floor was encased on both sides by high-gloss, mahogany wainscoting halfway up both sides of the hall wall. The handrailing and balustrade that ran along the upper length of the hall from the top of our stairs to the second-floor staircase matched the wood paneling. At the top right side of the staircase's second-floor landing, there was displayed, like a piece of artwork, a beautiful, rough-cut stained glass window, allowing no one to see in or out unless opened.

This stained glass window faced our neighbor to the right, and the side of their brick building was our view. There wasn't much space between Hungerford Street buildings. We had a regular see-through glass window in the hall that looked over the street. This window had been a door but converted when our second-floor front porch was removed. When I washed the windows standing on the front porch roof, Hungerford Street lay before me from one end of our section to the other, and I regretted again having no upper front porch. The porch would have been like a theater balcony to view scenes played out on Hungerford. Mom kept a full curtain on the hall window and placed a wooden stand with a drawer and space for books under it. When she was in her twenties, Grandma bought her a big hope chest. It would dominate the long wall between two of three doors that opened onto our front hall. Mother kept the hope chest filled with Grandmother's crochet work, extra sheets, blankets, and other bed finery. The smell of cedar climbed out when opened. She decorated its top with a ceramic vase holding multicolored plastic flowers and threw braided rugs in front of two of the three hall doors to decorate the space like a room. The door left of the chest led into the front room and the one on the right into the living room, the one at the head of the landing into a bedroom. We locked each door with a slender three-inch silver key. Door knobs were brass and each door built of solid wood with top and bottom panels. Quality building material and design weren't spared.

At the end of the hall left of the front window, a huge closet was provided to keep things. Clothing for a future season was stored there. Hobby paraphernalia, tennis rackets, ice skates, sleds, were kept there, too, as well as suitcases, boots, and household wares too many to accommodate inside our home. Next to the bedroom door stood my grandmother's polished, dark bamboo umbrella stand. The mahogany wood of stairs, molding, and handrailing duplicated itself on the four hall doors.

Our second-floor back porch, which gave us outdoor space to escape the heat of summer in a flat that had no air-conditioning, overlooked not only our yard but our neighbors' and beyond to the huge apartment blocks on Broad Street whose back porches faced ours and also the back verandas of a big apartment building on Grand Street. We had a rear window view of whatever the neighbors did. The views across the backyards from the porch were spectacular.

A big, white rocking chair hogged a lot of the back porch space where we could read, sit in the sun, or relax. My father loved the back porch to watch thunder and lightning storms like special effects on stage. Storms made Mom nervous. "Ellis, come in off the porch. That lightning is too close. You're going to get hit by it one day," was her advice to him. On hot summer nights in the backyard, we trapped fireflies in a bottle or watched them from the porch as they lit up the night, flitting over Grandma's lawn.

Daddy mowed the lawn with a mower that had no power but what he provided of his own. When he seeded it, he rolled over it with a huge cement roller my grandfather had made. Some yards, like the Cohens' and Duchaines', were spoiled by having been cut in half and gouged out for garages and driveways. They had minimal mowing. As no one in our family owned a vehicle, our backyard remained beautifully landscaped and not fractured by a driveway.

The cement roller on the right side of Mom and roses.

The huge, brown wooden garage that belonged to Mr. and Mrs. Cohen bordered the left side of our yard. Grandmother planted hostas and chrysanthemums near it so it looked pretty against the drab wood background, each complementing the other—flowers and wood.

Any yard in the Frog Hollow would find it difficult to compete with the one my grandmother created. It was as close to looking like a park as you could find anywhere in the city.

The lawn looked like a carpet and its entire length on each side boasted carefully cultivated flowerbeds and herbs.

An elegant weeping willow tree stood in the middle of the yard and under it one of two white wooden benches. Grandma bought and planted the young tree and it grew with me throughout the years. Years later it shaded the yard like a huge parasol. At the back end of the yard stood a trellis with roses growing over it. An ornate iron bird bath filled the center. Behind its bushes, a wonderful hidden area ran along the entire length of Hungerford Street's backyards. I could walk behind each neighbor's property unseen along this secluded back path all the way to Russ Street, passing the backyards of a dozen houses.

I write of the architectural structure of a building inside and out, discuss the building materials, and mention the appendages of front and back porches and the land it sits on. But I describe only a building, a structure. What I have to do is to add the rooms, the living space within each that created my home.

Our flat housed seven rooms and included a kitchen, a den, two bedrooms, a bathroom, a living room, and a front room. The size of each room was generous, and my mother exquisitely decorated each throughout the seventy-two years she lived there. Over and over, decade after decade, we could leave it and come back whether from school, church, holidays, street activities, beach or pool, and vacations. It stands, an anchor holding my memories in place in the Hollow on Hungerford. This venerable structure I called home has been without me for thirty-one years. I miss living there still.

Fun on a Neighborhood Street

Hungerford Street ran from Park to Capitol Avenue, but the middle of three parts, between Russ and Grand, was the section I lived on. Upon the stone sidewalks of this street, I played out my childhood. In the 1940s and 1950s, children rarely sat in on a sunny day, and the fresh air and sun shared the time outside with us. Hungerford became our playground. My mother didn't allow me in on a nice day. She pushed me outside. I eagerly went as did another twenty-eight children who shared this neighborhood street with me.

Sitting on the bottom stair of my front porch, I put on metal ball-bearing roller skates. Every kid back then, including me, mastered using them. I slipped each skate onto my shoes, tightened the strap, and most important, made sure the key tightened up the two prongs grasping each shoe. A strap secured the rest of the skate. Holding onto the handrailing, I carefully made my way from the stone slabs in front of the porch steps so as not to fall. I eased onto the sidewalk, my skating arena. The uneven walks had cracks of dirt, grass, and stones, making roller-skating a constant challenge. I watched for obstacles that could hamper my ride up the street. *Clicky clak, clicky clak*, the sound of ball-bearing wheels on the sidewalk was unique as they rolled over and over. If I went too fast, I had to grab something to stop. Not often, but enough times to recall, one of the two prongs holding the front of the shoe came free and the skate dragged along in back. I sat to put it back on. Gingerly, I learned to turn around on skates. I attempted nothing more daring than that. Not falling was the goal.

I not only rode on Hungerford's street, I also wrote on it. Hopscotch needed chalk to draw the eight squares for the game plus the turnaround or rest area at the top. I had a stone or button or something to toss into a square. If it landed in number one, I hopped on to number eight and then rested, turned around and made my way back to the start where the marker number one was picked up. I tossed it to the second square and so on. There were two areas of side-by-side numbers, and I could use both feet to straddle them and move on to the single ones, hopping on one foot. It was fun and good exercise. Our marked up sidewalks stayed sloppy until a rain washed away the chalk.

Then "Girls Are" marked up the street for a second popular game on Hungerford. Less restrictive, it had no numbers but subjects in each square. The squares at the beginning had "girls" and "boys" written in each box, and I used a ball to bounce around the squares reciting girls' or boys' names depending on which square I made it to. "Girls are: Jean, Jane, Joan," mostly began the game. If I made it back not stopping, I went on to the next category. There could be no interruption in reciting subjects, which could be colors, flowers, etc. Eight blocks made up this game too.

And then there was jump rope. Creating a sports gym outside, we had all manner of ropes. Some just a hard hunk of it and some bought with soft material and bound on each end with a red wooden handle. We jumped alone, holding both ends of the rope, or with two friends who held each end. From the single rope came the challenge of all challenges—double Dutch. Two sets of rope turned with double pieces in each of two girls' hands. The trick for them was not to tangle and stop the ropes. The jumper's challenge was to get inside the two twirling ropes without getting tangled in their revolutions. We each bent and swayed forward and backward, waiting for the right time to jump in. The jumps were counted. Those with the highest number won.

Sometimes I sat on a front porch or stood on the sidewalk for fun. Cards of all sorts were popular in my childhood and one was the trading card. They had on them myriad subjects including flowers, horses, dogs, cats, buildings, etc. I had a huge set and sometimes had duplicates to trade or just get rid of. I'd say, "Wanna trade? I'll trade you this card for that." And the bartering went on. But the cards we all loved and got in bubblegum packages for five cents were baseball ones. What we didn't realize then as we traded or flipped cards with Roger Maris or Ted Williams pictured on them, was that we held cards worth many dollars in decades to come. If only we had held on to them. Mom threw Dad's big collection away. Who knew? But one baseball shop owner told me, "If everyone held on to their collections, they wouldn't be worth anything today anyway." It put a perspective on my regret, but I never let Mom forget what she did.

The trading and baseball cards, too, could be flipped when not being swapped. I'd stand several along the bottom stair and with another card, try and knock down as many as I could. I held the card in between a second and third finger, flipping it with a wrist bend. The card walloped belonged to the kid hitting it. On Hungerford, everyone's porch steps at one time or another were used for the game. The cards we cared least about got used.

If the bottom of front porch stairs was not used to flip cards, then a ball would do. I threw the ball hoping to get it on the stair's edge, which was most difficult not only to hit but to catch as it returned quickly. I tossed balls, all manner of sizes, over and over for the thrill of a sport born on the streets that kept me and my friends outside. At times I went solo, tossing a ball at my own steps, but most play activity required one or more friends.

Not only did I roller skate, write, jump, barter, trade, flip, and bounce, but I dug around Hungerford Street. Whether backyard or side yard, my house or a playmate's, we all loved marbles. We dug a small hole to receive the marbles and smoothed the dirt around the hole so we'd have the best chance to get a marble in. The one with the most marbles in the pot won. I had a big collection of the round glass treasures but only played those I either had duplicates of or ones not pretty.

My grandmother's backyard looked like a park and visitors to it took in a breath when they saw the treasure hidden from the street. A walk to the back on a brick walk rimmed with greens and bushes took one through a rose-covered arbor that introduced the yard's entrance. Grandma's property was not gouged out with a parking lot as many of my friends' yards were. So among the expansive lawn, flowers, bushes, and weeping willow tree, there were myriad small branches whereby we fashioned bows and arrows. I picked a sturdy piece of tree branch, stripped off the leaves for the bow, and cut a slice on either end for a string. A series of narrower sticks were used for the arrows also stripped of growth. I shot here and there and mimicked the Indians I saw in the cowboy shows at the Lyric Theater on Saturday. My friends and I slunk from yards to streets shooting primitive homemade weapons at each other.

Our backyard's thick overhanging bushes also provided areas to create outdoor playhouses. Several of my girlfriends and I had our own place. Dolls and their furniture decorated those outdoor residences, and we visited each other across lawns. Back and forth, we strolled for visits with dolls in their carriages. One friend and I, not having enough doll clothes one summer, got them free at Woolworth's, one of two five-and-ten-cent stores on Park Street that stood side by side near the Immaculate Church rectory. We went downstairs, looked through the unlocked glass cases, and helped ourselves to what our dolls needed. We got adorable underclothes for them including tiny T-shirts.

A stroll, without the doll family, to the back of Grandma's yard, we hopped a wire fence and walked unimpeded all the way down to the end of Hungerford via the backs of neighbors' properties. It was an exciting activity, and I loved the secret, hidden way of the path. Nothing then was manicured, and most areas remained untouched, a paradise for me and all Hungerford Street's children. Not only the love of hidden paths but alleyways as well remain with me as an adult. In a city or town today, they are almost impossible to find again.

Sometimes I stood outside a friend's house and called out her name to signal I could play. The street was a magnet during summer vacation or on weekends, and most of us left our homes for the end-less play opportunities outside. Wherever we went, we all walked. No one had a bike when our age had a single digit. No one, that is, except little Mattie. He had a bike as small as he was, but it was the most wonderful bike we had seen. It was a two wheeler. My friends and I didn't have one, only a tricycle. We watched him zigzagging down the street on his wheels. We could ride his bike. We could ride it for a nickel. No one begged harder for the five cents than I did, and I managed a ride or two during the course of the summer. Everyone coveted that little bike, and Mattie began his entrepreneurial career on Hungerford, waiting for eager customers to pay up. What a thrill to ride and not walk past neighborhood homes.

We only had a tricycle.

There wasn't a kid on Hungerford who didn't adore ice cream. We bought Dixie cups from Harold and Millie's store on the corner of Grand and Hungerford. The small cup came with a prepackaged wooden spoon. It wasn't only the ice cream that delighted us but the Dixie cup cover as well. At one time, each lid bore the picture of a famous movie star, and we stood around as each licked, hoping for a new one to add to our collections. If we already had the star we got that day, we traded it for one we didn't have. A Dixie cup cover then could be exciting and even start a collection.

Some of the fun we had wasn't all innocent, wasn't all Dick and Jane. We became fascinated with matches and cigarettes. Around our homes, it would have been impossible to try either. But there was one area on Hungerford Street, near Grand, that held possibilities to be naughty—the lot Fannie's grocery store sat on. Dirt and overgrown bushes covered the property, and we found hiding places to try the matches and cigarettes under the brush. We never injured ourselves and for that, luck was with us.

Mattie may have had a bike but Tom had a list of his favorite girlfriends in order of how much he liked them. He nailed up a weekly copy of his list and posted it on a telephone pole near my friend Carol's house. Oh, how we girls approached it with trepidation, expectation, and hope that we had climbed higher in Tom's esteem since the last posting. I rose to number four one time and was thrilled. Tom lived in the block and had a sister. He wasn't especially popular in the neighborhood, but that list lifted him socially higher, made him more popular than I believe he thought he would ever be.

It wasn't always a hot, sunny summer day on Hungerford Street when we had fun but it could be a cold winter one as well. The city didn't plow Hungerford Street or any street immediately after it snowed. The city took its time and was more laid-back plowing. The snow lay on the road long after it fell, and cars pressed it down to a flat, hard surface as tires rolled over and over it. What a beautiful sight. Sled in hand, looking down Hungerford's winter-white street, running as fast as I could in boots, I dropped to the road on my Flyer sled, hoping for as long a ride as I could get before I got up and repeated the process. I can still feel the impact, the *thud*, as my sled and I fell to the road for the ride.

We built ice forts block by block with the cold snow, and they resembled igloos when finished. Several of us built the forts with entrances large enough to crawl into and sit. The trick was to get the structure to stay up. We crawled in, my friends and I, and sat and chatted in that freezing icehouse. I chill up today recalling the times. One we built in my backyard, but another was built in the evening hours on Hungerford right in front of our house. I remember looking up at the blue Christmas lights in our second-floor bay window. The street-light cast a glow on the whole winter scene. The evening was peaceful. I don't recall the circumstances whereby I was allowed out in the darker hour. But the memory persists of that one peaceful winter night in an igloo on Hungerford.

From summers through winters, with no machinery, no technical devices, in the days of my childhood in the 1940s and 1950s, we, Hungerford Street children, created simple fun that kept us out playing on our street. We didn't know then it wouldn't always be like that for kids. Later, streets would be empty of children, now inside sitting with TVs, computers, iPads, and other social media gadgets. One hears no sound from them, and the noise of our play yesterday drowns out the stillness of today.

The Rock and Roll Collection

T he 1954 Decca recording "Rock Around The Clock" by Bill Haley and His Comets, we kids thought began the rock-and-roll era. In retrospect it didn't, but most historians agree that more than any other song, it brought the rock-and-roll era into the main music culture in the United States and around the world.

Mad about music in the 1950s, that decade took me from age eight to seventeen, rock and roll and me, both youngsters. I loved the rock beat, the black sound, and just popular music so different from the 1940's softer, slower, sentimental sound. On Saturday morning, one Connecticut radio station played the top pop hits starting with 100 and working its way to number 1. The top songs were dictated by *Billboard's* list of the most played by radio disc jockeys, bought in record shops, or played in jukeboxes. I sat in a rocking chair for hours in our huge front room, mahogany wall doors closed. Most single records played were about two and a half minutes, and I sang along with each. No one bothered me on those early weekend mornings. I learned the words to each and every song so could sing along with the vocalist, lyrics committed for life. Some of the early records I owned included songs and artists popular before and a short time during the 1950s rock-and-roll era and included Kay Starr, Frankie Lane, Bing Crosby, and the Four Aces. Even one of my cowboy heroes from the Lyric kiddie show, Gene Autry, had a 1950 Christmas hit "Rudolph the Red-Nosed Reindeer." The earlier low-key crooner music would never be a favorite of mine even at an early age and didn't entice me onto a dance floor. But it was rock-and-roll singers and their new beat songs which made it impossible not to want to get up and bebop along with the music. With poodle skirt over crinoline slip, twirling, feet in white buck or saddle shoes, flying, clasping a partner's hand, and getting twirled in circles under his arm, pulling together and then apart, I lived to dance. Everything in the 50s was rock and roll and dancing on radio and television.

In 1952, when I turned ten, American Bandstand debuted on ABC with a twenty-two-year-old host, Dick Clark. He kept the show going for twenty years. Television grew in popularity by 1954. I danced to Bandstand's music with the rest of America's youngsters while watching the fledgling clean-cut teenage stars dancing on television. Girls in full skirts and tight hair curls, and boys in shirts and slacks and oftentimes ties—neat attire on those TV teens. We had our favorites, and they became celebrities to us. TV competed with radio to promote songs and singers.

It wasn't enough to listen and learn the great 1950s songs, I had to own them as well. I'd boast 221 45s in my mostly rock-and-roll-era collection. The first sixty records I bought were recorded in the 1950s.

At first, I thought to collect only the large 78rpm records and not the smaller 45s. I bought the first one at the Belmont record shop housed in a two-story building on the corner of Washington Street near Park. A shop dedicated to selling music, it was also a meeting place for many of us kids from Hungerford Street who, with me, often took the fifteen-minute walk to the Belmont. I could go in, put earphones on, listen to my selection in one of several small booths, and maybe buy the record. There was no time limit. If I liked the song, I bought the record, but sales people at this music mecca never got cranky if I didn't buy. A booth wasn't always available so I waited. My first purchase, a 78 rpm record, I lavished love and care on—too much of each. I cleaned it over and over until it cracked in half. Not only was my first record broken but my heart too. I decided to go with the smaller 45s which were impossible to fracture. Some of the labels even pronounced them unbreakable. They were my kind of records.

I didn't always buy new records like I did at the Belmont. My mother and father rarely had money to spend on such frills. But I had another option to amass a collection—a huge warehouse way up on Park Street near Main. Its cavernous floor held long wooden tables on which were piled high used 45 rpms. These seconds from jukeboxes, I could purchase for a dime. I spent hours during summer vacation from Burns picking through the endless piles of records with some of my Hungerford Street pals also getting a collection together. I often left with a half dozen records. During two summers, 1956 and 1957, I worked tobacco and, with some of the money I earned, added to my collection.

I kept my first seventy-five records in a square, red box which held the small 45s. It measured eight-inch square. A red plastic handle on top, brass closure in front, and two brass hinges in back decorated it. The label pronounced the box an Amfile Platter Pak phonograph record case number 750 and a quality product.

Inside the case were seventy-five numbered dividers to index, label, and separate each record. With the dividers, simple, easy filing, and quick finding were promised. Also included was a pullout cardboard threefold sheet and numbered 1–75 to write in each record's information. The sheet had four columns: one for a file number that was already prenumbered 1–75, the second for the manufacturer's number, the third for title, and the fourth for the artist. The threefold sheet accommodated not only the hit song's information but a second line for the flip side's mostly unpopular song as well. I could then record 150 songs on the trifold cardboard and didn't need to refer to the 8 sentences of directions on its use as the procedure was Dick and Jane easy.

Most of my records I got at the Park Street warehouse. I waited for those ten-cent jukebox reruns. But the jackets of most records bought there were generic beige ones. The covers didn't match the record company labeled on the record itself. Had I been putting the collection together today, I might have matched them better as I did have jackets that I could match to records. The jackets put on at the warehouse were put on records indiscriminately. No one cared if they matched. Some jackets, like the record itself, had the record company logo on them like RCA with its Victrola and Nipper the dog label. It was on this label that Elvis recorded all his songs from 1956. Myriad label colors, like those found in a Crayola crayon box, distinguished each recording company, and it seemed few colors duplicated themselves on a competitor's recording. There were twenty-eight different labels and about a dozen differing label colors just within the seventy-five records I kept in the red box. Some with the same color differentiated themselves in another shade. Decca had a black label; Coral, an orange; Capitol, purple; Columbia, red; and King, blue, to mention a few. But the most famous in retrospect was the yellow Sun label manufactured in Memphis, Tennessee. It was simple, with nine label ID entries, whereas most records had fifteen or more. I would count three Sun labels in my collection. The collection also included eleven picture jackets; three of them in the first seventy-five records in the red carry box. One of the first three was Elvis's "Hound Dog" with its flip side of "Don't Be Cruel." I contradict myself by a previous assertion that most records didn't have a hit on its second side as both sides of this particular record were equally popular. A cardboard extended play (four songs on the record) by Elvis shares the box's space with a picture jacket of Pat Boone, also with a dual side hit.

The record jacket would also prove most valuable as years aged my collection, which today is sixty-four years old. The jacket picture of Elvis, who only sang on the RCA label on that dual-sided recording of "Hound Dog" and "Don't Be Cruel," displayed him with long, unkempt, greasy hair and clutching a microphone. Elvis came onto the major US music scene in 1956, the same year I first worked in the tobacco fields and sheds and saw his picture tacked up onto a shed beam. He became the king of rock and roll during my second tobacco summer in 1957. Pat Boone, popular at the time, presented a contrast to Elvis, what with white buck shoes, cardigan, and neatly combed hair. One popular record debuting in 1958, "Sixteen Candles" by the Crests, was also my age that year.

The initial seventy-five records in the collection, I stored in the red carry case. The other loose 146 45s had to be content piled in the corner of a living room cabinet. There were some finds among that warehouse pile, including a Sun label with songs by Jerry Lee Lewis accompanied by his wild-thumping piano playing, two picture jackets of Elvis's recordings, one of Chubby Checker on the Parkway label, and a cardboard one when Buddy Holly still sang with the Crickets on Brunswick, a subsidiary of Decca records. They all became part of my collection inventory. The eleven picture jackets in the collection include four extended plays, the latter always of cardboard.

The old standard 78 record seemed old-fashioned in the 1950s, and everyone wanted to own the latest craze—the 45s and something to play them on. One record jacket had printed on it the following:

"This record can be played only on 45 rpm instruments." Throughout the first decade of rock and roll, I owned a few record players. They weren't expensive and closed, looked like small suitcases. There was a protruding metal piece in the center but could only accommodate the tiny hole of the 75 and 33 1/3 rpms. The 45s had a center hole one and a half inches, so each record player came with either a tall stack piece to play ten records continuously without having to manually change each or small individual plastic inserts to use for the individual 45s. There were eight or so different kinds of insert discs, and I owned three. Each disc fit perfectly into the 45 record center. If ever I changed a needle, I don't recall. The simple, mono record player was upgraded to a high fidelity, nicknamed hi-fi, and then to a stereophonic player in 1958. We shortened its name to stereos.

The records that came through the decades without scratches, without warping, were those I didn't like and seldom played—the reverse side of the hit one. These songs weren't played in jukeboxes either. Records I loved and which gave the most joy had the wounds of overplay from the simple record players with unchanged needles. No one expected to hold onto the collection for the future, but I did.

I bought my first twenty records in 1955 at thirteen. The music began then, continued, and never died. Those 1950s rock-and-roll songs remained memorized to sing again even in a new music era that looks back with me, nostalgic for the grand era of rock and roll.

The Film Star Collection

My film star collection was a passion and hobby that consumed my free time for decades at a frenzy that had no parallel, not even the rock-and-roll collection. I adored movie stars, loved their films, lives, children, and I knew them better than I did most of my neighbors, including Mr. and Mrs. Cohen. And so I channeled my love into a film star collection that began in grammar school when I was eleven and continued throughout high school and a decade beyond. Unlike the rock-and-roll collection which required only that I buy the records and store them in a box, the film star collection was manually intensive and had to be created. In sixteen years (1953–1969) I finished most of it. I had no idea then what a good thing it was I worked at the nonstop pace I did, as my time to collect was quickly ending, the clock running out.

Like the rock-and-roll collection, the early film star collection began in something red; this time a scrapbook. The first scrapbook I began in 1953 was of thick back and front cardboard covers held together with a decorative string tied through two small plastic holds. The script across the front cover left no question as to what the book was—a "Scrap Book." Within its forty-eight pages, I pasted a cornucopia of picture types representing the eighty-two scrapbooks in the collection. This first one—a microcosm of them all.

At eleven, I used little rhyme or reason in the artistic creation of the first scrapbook. A few pages had the same star's pictures on them, but most pages were a mishmash of different stars, some in color, black and white, pictures cut from movie magazines and other magazine publications, newspapers, and even a card, all meshed together in a hodgepodge. Actors, actresses, stars with their children, full-page colored pictures of one star and full pages of black-and-white pictures, myriad smaller ones in color and black and white, all possibilities for picture types were pasted in this introductory first try. Unlike the rock-and-roll collection for which I bought records and stored them in a box, this film star one was manual and required materials to buy and tools to use.

Pictures in later scrapbooks I cut ruler straight and held them on with LePage's Grip Spreader Mucilage, a ritzy name for glue. Its reddish rubber top sat on the container like a cap. I pierced it carefully to release the glue and not make the hole too big so that the glue ran out, leaving me no control of the amount spread on each picture. It was an art to put just enough on each corner, and I mastered the procedure early. It wasn't enough to smear each corner, but care had to be given to do the edge points so they didn't stick up. Cutting and pasting was sloppy in this first try. In page sides, that first scrapbook was thin compared to later ones as I hadn't yet bought filler pages that could be untied, taken apart, and expanded with extra sheets.

Under many pictures in scrapbook number one, I printed in pencil and crayon each star's name if it wasn't preprinted. Being in grammar school was reflected in this first scrapbook try. Some names had green crayon lines under them too. They were my favorites in 1953 and included William Holden, Deborah Kerr, Fernando Lamas, Rhonda Fleming, and Eleanor Parker. I used crayons not only to write in names and underline favorites but also to color in black-and-white pictures. Included in several I colored was a picture of Liz Taylor wrapped in a curtain, which I changed to yellow, and added yellow to Janet Leigh's otherwise uncolored hair in a shot of her with Robert Wagner. Three other actresses became blond with my yellow Crayola crayon. I outlined in blue a picture of Bob Wagner and another in purple of Rhonda Fleming. I was more casual with this first creation. I'd become fussy and exacting, putting later ones together as my mastery of the art of the scrapbook increased with age.

I'd stop enhancing my scrapbooks with script and color after the twelfth one. My star worship continued throughout the 1950s and extended decades beyond. Even as these stars aged, I continued to glue their pictures into my endless scrapbooks.

In Grandma's cellar in the small closet under the stairs is where I kept some of the earlier scrapbooks, including this first one, which stubbornly held on to the musty basement smell of the dirt floor that had no acquaintance with sun or fresh air.

I didn't just happen to buy a movie magazine and a scrapbook in 1953. I went to the Lyric movie theater often in the early 1950s, and that was enough for my fill of film stars. I hadn't planned on beginning a collection. That resulted from a reprimand one summer day over six decades ago.

Mother adored the sun and wanted me in it as much as possible whether at Hammonasset Beach or around the neighborhood. Just as playing under the boardwalk at Hammonasset was unacceptable, so, too, was spending it indoors one glorious summer day with my Lithuanian friend, Ely. The huge, long residential apartment block on Hungerford held many residences and in one, Ely, her parents, and two brothers lived. My friend had no film star collection either but loved movies stars as I did. In a block apartment basement, cold and damp as my grandmother's, we found a big box of movie soundtrack records. Kids that we were, the find was interesting but nothing was done with it save an excited examination. Memory has erased any recollection of which soundtracks they were. We spent a long time on that beautiful day in the basement looking for other treasures. I had no idea that Mother was looking for me and was she mad! When Ely and I came out, she called me home, very upset. She rarely hollered at me and later felt bad. I would use her guilt to my advantage. Coincidentally, we were going to the movies at the Lyric later that evening, and I told her that earlier in the week I had seen a movie magazine I liked and wondered if I could buy it. In the 1950s, the magazines cost twenty-five cents each. On the way to the theater, I got my first one at Aunt Millie's store. My collection had begun.

The reprimand had been worth it. I was on my way that day toward amassing a huge movie star collection.

Most magazines I bought, some were given to me. The popular ones in the 1950s included *Photoplay, Modern Screen,* and *Screen Stories.* Each was published once a month, and I was at one of several Hartford drugstores to get a copy the day one came out. I couldn't wait for the next issue, and its release date was published in the magazine before. If I tore the pictures out to paste in a scrapbook, I lost a half inch or so of them. So I took out the staples that held the pages together and pulled the magazine apart so as not to lose any part of a picture, especially the full-paged colored ones. The wooden kitchen table in our second-floor flat on Hungerford Street was my workplace, scissors and glue, my tools. I pasted to the pre- rock-and -roll tunes popular on the radio that first year of 1953 like Patti Page's "(How Much Is) That Doggie in the Window?" and Tony Bennett's "Rags to Riches" and Jonie James's "Your Cheatin' Heart."

The scrapbooks themselves included half a dozen kinds bought in five-and-ten-cent stores or larger establishments like Grant's or Bradlees. That first scrapbook held with the string woven through two plastic holders measured 12 3/4" × 11 1/4" with rough page edges. There were twenty-three pages for a total of forty-six sides. I could use the two cover backs for forty-eight possible pages. I didn't waste an inch of space. I would total five of this particular scrapbook type, numbers six, eight, fifty-nine, sixty, and including number one.

Another scrapbook type similar to the first red one but smaller (10" × 12") had the cardboard front and back covers, plastic to thread the string to hold it, and "Scrap Book" written on it too. It had a few more pages (thirty-one) and sides (sixty-two) plus use of the two back covers. I'd put pictures into eleven of this type.

Later with scrapbooks held by removable string, I could buy filler pages to insert after the scrapbook was untied and taken apart. The extra sheets made for a thicker scrapbook to accommodate more pictures.

The scrapbook that made up the bulk of the collection, however, was published by the Whitman Company out of Racine, Wisconsin.

It was longer than the hardcover ones, 13" × 3/8" but shared the same 10" width. It also numbered thirty-one pages so sixty-two sides to use plus the two covers if I chose. It could not, however, be taken apart to add pages. This scrapbook had a thinner cover and page material. The covers were unique and came in sundry prints including the *Ding Dong School*, Rock Hudson, Mickey Mouse (with a pink cover color and one with orange), *The Lone Ranger*, and three bucolic scenes. This scrapbook type made up forty-two of the eighty-two.

The heart and soul, the bulk of my film star collection, was housed in those eighty-two scrapbooks. Three quarters of them, about sixty, I completed in the 1950s, beginning with that first one in 1953. In seven years, I put together sixty, averaging eight and a half scrapbooks a year during the 1950s when I began assembling in my kitchen workshop. Some, like number thirty-seven, I finished in a day. Eighteen scrapbooks I created in the 1960s and the last five in later years, very slowly and spaced years apart. By then, movie magazines were no longer published and stars were more reticent to expose their personal lives to the public. Each succeeding scrapbook from that first red one in the summer of 1953 became neater and lovelier, more artistically put together. From this combo, I branched out and differentiated with similar picture types and sources as the years went by.

The bulk of the eighty-two, however, were combo scrapbooks, their contents a hodgepodge in that they were, like the first one, black-and-white pictures or colored in all possible sizes and included actors and actresses and their children, who looked up from the pages of the myriad sources of their pictures. I would change the scrapbook format eight times.

I'd make scrapbooks of just one picture type different from the combo's many types that might include just actresses, just actors, all black and white, all color, or those made up of only newspaper articles. In the 1950s, newspapers such as the *Hartford Courant* and *Hartford Times* featured movie stars and covered their films, travel, weddings, and their children. Stars' lives got press often.

Besides those five varieties of combo, I'd make scrapbooks with pictures of just one star and these included three for Grace Kelly, who, in 1956, married a French prince; nine for Elizabeth Taylor; one for Paul Newman; one for Greta Garbo; and half a scrapbook that Garbo shared with Gary Cooper. I accumulated pictures of each star until I had enough to make a scrapbook.

Another variation of the combo besides the six was the creation of sections of one star with at least ten or more pages within a combo scrapbook, and these included four sections of Grace Kelly; ten for Ingrid Bergman (who had returned from exile in Europe to the US in 1956 and earned an Oscar the same year); one for Tab Hunter; five for Elizabeth Taylor; one for Rock Hudson; two for Clark Gable; one for Bob Wagner and Natalie Wood; and one for Troy Donahue. Debbie Reynolds, Patricia Neal, and Mia Farrow also had a section within one of the scrapbooks.

Then there was the eighth scrapbook type—just the children of stars. I loved their offspring, some of whom would go on to become films stars in their own right such as Carrie Fisher, Miguel Ferrer, Jamie Lee Curtis, Jane Fonda, and Candice Bergen. I put together three huge ones and thought the older son of Elizabeth Taylor one of the most beautiful of Hollywood's children, and in a short story I wrote in grammar school, I based the main character on him.

The first picture of Elvis, the one I saw in the tobacco barn in the summer of 1956 when I first worked the fields, is in the scrapbook numbered ten, put together that year.

Scrapbook number twenty-six, I did in September of 1957. I began it in Hartford Hospital, where I went for an emergency appendectomy. I had just begun my second year of high school. I hadn't felt well in class so the teacher sent me home. Dr. Elliot, our family doctor who practiced out of an office on Park Street, came to our home and pain from pressure on my right side told him I needed the surgery and quickly. My mother brought pictures, scrapbook, and glue to the hospital, so I would have something to do while I recuperated.

Another notation indicated that scrapbook number thirty-nine included mostly pictures I had gotten from *Life* magazines given to me by my friend Beverly. They covered the years 1954–1955. Beverly was the daughter of Mrs. Cherwinski of the Clothesline memoir chapter.

In December of 1958, after using forty-two Whitman scrapbooks, I received a big hardcover one as a Christmas present from my family. After five years of collecting and making scrapbooks, they realized how important this hobby was to me. It was number fifty-two, and I finished it in four months. Elvis, within its pages, is pictured in the army and stationed in Germany.

Esther Williams was a B actress and swimming star I liked because I wanted to swim like her. She stroked through the water with a grace I envied and hoped my Pope Park lessons would create out of me a swimmer like her. She did the Australian crawl or freestyle stroke with her head out of the water, an improper form, but was graceful when she did it.

After buying movie magazines, cutting them up, and pasting film stars pictures into scrapbooks, three years into my collection assembly, Hollywood, its set and stars, came to me. To Connecticut that is, Chester, Connecticut, where the longtime popular Doris Day and Jack Lemmon film, *It Happened to Jane*, was to be filmed. At fourteen, I had no driver's license, so I scrambled to get a ride to Chester. My girlfriend, Ely, had her cousin drive us. I was so excited to meet two very popular stars and favorites of mine, especially Doris Day. Whereas I liked Lemmon, my mother adored him. The drive from Hartford that beautiful, hot day in August took about an hour. We landed in the center of Chester's Main Street, right in the middle of Day doing a scene. I managed fourteen black-and-white snapshots of her. I was disappointed that Lemmon wasn't shooting that day. Day was gracious after her scene shoot and stopped to chat with us and sign autographs. She introduced to us her then husband and manager, Marty Melchner. I was meeting my first star, and she didn't disappoint. She was gracious and as lovely in person as she was on screen and in my scrapbooks.

And then I welcomed to Connecticut, five years later and eight years into my collection, another film star—Troy Donahue. Tall, blue-eyed, blond, and so handsome, he was a heartthrob of my sister, Jan, and me and the rest of the teens in the States. He arrived to film *Parrish* in Windsor and my sister and I excitedly awaited him. I had read the Mildred Savage book of the same title even before I knew a film would be made because its theme was the Connecticut tobacco industry. I had worked tobacco a second summer only four years before. So that June date in 1961, when Hollywood once again came to Connecticut, Jan and I made the twenty-minute walk through Bushnell Park to the Hilton Hotel where it was advertised Troy was staying. What luck! Jan and I saw him inside the Hilton Hotel lobby in a casual outfit, talking to someone. I snapped his photo. We returned a second time and met him coming out of the hotel. We talked to him. He was formally dressed that day. I took another picture of him. He, like Doris Day, was gracious and signed an autograph to Jan. He also remarked to her, "What a wonderful voice you have." It was her defining feature, that deep-throated voice.

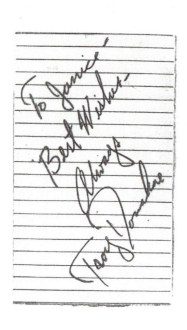

As the years passed, I attended lots of theater productions in Connecticut and New York if one of my beloved stars was featured. Many of the great stars of yesteryear, like Joan Fontaine, Tyrone

Power, Ingrid Bergman, and Bette Davis, appeared on stage as their silver screen days ended.

Six decades later, the town of Chester would celebrate the film Doris Day and Jack Lemmon made, and I attended, taking with me for their historical society, copies of the fourteen pictures I took; four pages about the film and five pages of advertising for the event in the *Shoreline* paper. Into antique frames, I would put two enlargements of my own black-and-white pictures and from a scrapbook, copy an 8 1/2" × 11" colored picture of Day from 1956. E. M. Lowes Theater in Hartford showed the film, and I copied four of the ads for it from the newspaper. I accompanied the collection, most put into a photograph album for them, with a talk about how I accumulated the different pictures. The Chester Historical Society sent me a written thank-you that officially entered my gift into their archives.

Fittingly, my final scrapbooks are of stars' obituaries. Film stars after the 1950s rarely got into newspapers or magazines until they died. The more famous and influential the star had been to show business, the more coverage. The sticker on the gray cover of the first obit one, I bought for eight dollars in Bradlees, one of several large department stores in Connecticut. Because the collection is still intact, I can compare scrapbook prices.

These final scrapbooks are bittersweet as with each death, I felt I had lost a friend. I had pasted pictures of them from the beginning to the end of their careers and saw these friends now old and fading. At the end of their careers, they hid from cameras and stayed off movie sets. And, having seen and now owning their films in hundreds of VHS tapes when they starred at the pinnacle of success, it was a shock when they died because I had left them in a perennial time warp in my mind and heart.

The last scrapbook I bought for the obits cost fourteen dollars, a far cry from the twenty-five-cent ones I bought six decades before. This scrapbook accommodates pictures on 100 pages, 102 using the front and back covers and measures 11 3/4" × 14".

In a bureau drawer upstairs in my Clinton home, where residual film star material was stored for years, I found a book with 150 cards of Elvis Presley sold in packs of twelve, each card held within a 2 1/2" × 3 1/2" plastic pocket.

In the same drawer, a red scrapbook that aptly says "Photographs" on its front cover in script, contains one hundred plus glossy 8 1/2" × 11" prints of Greta Garbo, mostly scenes from her talkies films, but some posed studio shots. I paid twenty-five cents for each picture, which I sent away for. Most came from the firm Stephen Sally that dealt with selling the glossies. Recently, I gave an introductory talk before a film of Garbo's was shown at Saybrook's Acton Library. The film was *Anna Karenina*, and I accompanied the talk about this Swedish actress who left the film industry before I was born, with three framed pictures and seven pasted on thick cardboard, all scenes from the film.

The same drawer held an accumulation of fourteen years (2003–2016) of newspaper obituaries, including those of Bob Hope, Katharine Hepburn, Paul Newman, Elizabeth Taylor, Marlon Brando, all needing to be pasted into a second and third obit scrapbook. These stars were giants of the film industry.

There are also in that drawer a couple of sets of star card games and three boxes of newspaper prints of film scenes advertising what was playing at the fifteen or so movie theaters in Hartford. The ads told which films were held over, and in the mix was a drive-in movie ad. This collection numbers about 1,500 of those newspaper prints. Four hundred movie magazines dating from the 1940s and sixty books including hardcover and paperbacks, biographies, autobiographies, and history of film, make up another part of the collection. There are also three more scrapbooks of photograph stills from Steven Sally.

And then one day, the screen fades to black. It's over. The great star system that fueled the building of local movie theaters where I watched film after film; the end of movie magazines in which I saw and read about luxurious lives that mimicked film roles; the death of the legends upon which the industry had thrived. All are gone but saved in eighty-two scrapbooks and countless other appendages of a collection that brings them back and captures them when they lived, when they worked, and displayed glamour and beauty and as many styles of acting as there were performers. In a darkened theater like the Lyric, they took me, my family, and friends out of our ordinary lives for an hour or two. I miss them. I didn't realize all too soon it would be "The End."

One day the stars were gone.

The Lyric Theater

Every Saturday at high noon, an usher threw open the doors of our small Park Street movie theater, the Lyric, releasing us, the neighborhood kids, onto the streets again.

After sitting in a darkened theater for two hours, being out was like resuming our lives again—like life was on hold, part of it having gone by for the time we sat through the Saturday matinee. We spilled out and scattered north, east, south, and west, as if each of us held a different compass. We had shared the Wild West with a bunch of celluloid cowboy heroes at the Saturday morning Lyric kiddie show in Hartford.

The B westerns, most made in the 1940s, theater owners reserved to show kids on Saturday morning. For a ten-cent ticket, another for the best popcorn I have ever tasted, a bunch of friends, my sister, and I could watch cowboy heroes and their sidekicks ride around ranges and ranches, valleys and prairies, saving poor farmers, local cattlemen, and underdogs; they settled water and grazing rights, gold and silver claims, feuds and fights by exposing land swindlers and city slickers and restoring tranquility. The fast-riding cowboys risked themselves for justice and played the drama out to a soundtrack of gunfire and hoofbeats. In the end, good triumphed and our heroes rode their horses into the sunset but returned for the next Saturday morning matinee.

Roy Rogers and Dale Evans, Hopalong Cassidy, Gene Autry, the Lone Ranger, Red Ryder, and Little Beaver dominated the western silver screen. My sister, Jan, had a crush on the Indian boy, Little Beaver, and every time he showed up in the film's preview, we'd tease her; "Oh, there's Little Beaver. Jan likes Little Beaver," we'd whisper.

She hated that. I would see every western ever made, including the cartoons and *Movietone News* that went with the Saturday morning double features. We got a lot for our dime in the 1950's.

If you asked me how far from our tenement the Lyric was, I'd tell you, "It's only a block and a half away, not even a ten-minute walk."

The three-story red brick Lyric Theater building occupied 585 Park—just a spot on the mile-long commercial and residential street. Designed by Edward T. Wiley of Hartford and built in 1928, the Lyric took up the left-hand side, near the corner of Park and Broad Streets, south side. Suspended over the sidewalk like a roof, the projecting theater marquee was held up by half a dozen thick wires that kept it secured. The two sides of the marquee displayed Lyric in bold letters and the front, Now Showing, with the names of the current features. Our small theater showed second run films. For first runs, you went downtown to the Lowe's Poli, the Strand, or one of several other larger movies houses. The signboard interrupted the otherwise flat lines of the buildings flanking it, including the taller Collins building to the Lyric's left.

With its white band course above the first and third floors, together with a white stone modillion course that made its way under the theater's cornice, the Lyric was pretty. White keystones and two stone wreaths that draped themselves over a medallion, together with a center window with a stone arch above it, were architectural gildings of this lily.

The clerk selling tickets occupied a small, narrow glass booth at the entrance. She seemed jailed at least until we were all in.

The tickets were collected in the lobby just outside the inner entrance doors. Eleven-by-fourteen inch posters of the current show and ones for coming attractions decorated the lobby walls. The Technicolor stills remained displayed under a locked glass case safe from souvenir collectors.

Joe, a short, balding Italian American, lived with his wife in a tenement a few doors down from the Lyric and worked as the theater's manager. He often let my family and me in free during the week. He'd say, "Go ahead," and wave us by.

I so wanted three of the Lyric's publicity stills one year, and Joe gave them to me. I still have them—two from Gary Cooper's 1956 film *The Hanging Tree* and one from Rock Hudson's 1958 *Written on the Wind*. I'm glad Joe ignored the disclaimer on the three posters that read, "Property of National Screen Service Corp. Licensed for display only in connection with the exhibition of this picture at your theatre. Must be returned immediately thereafter." These display stills accompanied the double features that changed every Wednesday and Sunday, but those three were the only ones I could talk him out of.

The narrow front entrance of the Lyric gave no impression of the three sections of long rows of seats and huge stage beyond it. Once inside, passing the glass showcases of the concession stand with its infinite snack offerings, the structure turned right and took itself around the back of several shops on Broad Street.

The aisles were red rugged but not under the seats. And good thing because at the end of every show, gum, popcorn, Cracker Jacks, candy pieces, and myriad wrappers and napkins from our film feast lined the floors where we sat and had to be removed before actors and their leading ladies could entertain the next audience. I hated it when I walked someone's chewing gum home on my shoe bottom. The wrapped Cracker Jack toy found at the bottom of the box always created a flurry of activity. You had to eat through the molasses-glazed popcorn and peanuts to get to it. And then say—"Look what I got" or "What'd you get?" We leaned over to show our prize and maybe swap for a better one. "Wanna trade?" we whispered. The Cracker Jack box and paper the prize was wrapped in joined the rest of the junk on the floor.

If you didn't want to sit downstairs, the Lyric offered a balcony. But the place had a reputation for accommodating older kids going steady and who spent most of the time necking or something. I sat there a few times. It was like sitting in another theater. I was used to looking up and not down on the screen. I belonged downstairs.

Sometimes the Lyric hosted giveaways on its stage of dark, open red curtains that flanked it like heavy velvet gowns. Then, some of the audience took center stage. The lucky number on your ticket stub got you a prize. One year I won a little wooden rocking chair painted with bright colors. The chair looked Mexican. But there was a trade-off. I had to go on the stage to get it. When the manager called my number, I couldn't believe it. I was happy but terrified. I dreaded going up to fetch my prize. But I did. The walk seemed miles long, going by endless rows of audience that seemed to stare at me with one gigantic eye. I still have the little chair, repainted and reseated though it is. It was worth walking the gauntlet to get it.

Dinnerware collections were sold in the lobby, and every week you could buy one piece. We never got a whole set, just what Mom needed to serve meals to Dad, my sister, and me. One set offered was a blue-and-white one called Blue Willow, the other, a pale-yellow one with flowers and colonial scenes on it.

The Lyric hosted those giveaways but sometimes wanted something from us. The theater collected for different worthwhile charities including the March of Dimes. When the theater lit up for intermission, the usher announced a collection. He walked to the front aisle and passed a bucket along each row and waited for it to return to him like a slow-moving boomerang. He watched it like some out of place sheriff guarding a portable bank where only deposits were allowed.

An usher with a flashlight patrolled the aisles during the matinees to make sure we all behaved. Sometimes, when it sounded like the performers whispered, I made a trip to the back of the theater where the usher stood to tell him the sound was too low.

I supplemented hours at the Saturday morning matinees with many spent during a weekday evening or Sunday afternoon at the Lyric with my parents and sister. Sometimes my grandmother came. She loved Bing Crosby and Rosemary Clooney. She called him Bing and her, Rosemary Caloon. We all adored movies.

We didn't buy Lyric popcorn during these family excursions. To save money, we popped our own in a big, dented aluminum pan with a flat cover that always had a residue of butter left on it when the popping stopped. I poured popcorn kernels onto bubbling butter at the bottom of the overused pan and waited for the first kernels to jump, a signal the rest could now be slowly shaken back and forth, back and forth over the gas flames. Slow to start, I quickened the rate the more the kernels exploded and banged against the underside of the aluminum cover as if anxious to be out. Sometimes if I added too many kernels, the popped corn heaved the cover up to spill out over the gas stove burner and little flames had to be put out. There was no need for more butter as the kernels, having been popped in it, clung to our exploded pieces, tinting each a golden yellow. One pan filled a sandwich bag.

And the sandwich bags we carried, shiny with the grease spots from the drying butter, were a giveaway our popcorn was homemade, and we walked confidently in with it. In the fifties, no one cared if you brought your own.

I remember the year colored popcorn kernels came out, and the red, blue, and green treat was a delight. The fad didn't last long though. We also sat through the 3-D craze in the 1950s. Using polarized glasses with their light cardboard frames, conspicuous around the dark plastic of the glasses, we looked weird sitting there, look-alikes in our artificial specs.

Mom saved money buying candy in one of the five-and-ten-cent stores across the street from the Lyric. For a nickel you got a Hershey or Nestle Crunch bar and for a nickel more, an Almond Joy. But I loved Ju Ju Fruits. I squashed them and kept them in my hand to soften. Jan called the pink-and-white licorice Good and Plenty her favorite.

The Lincoln Dairy also shared Park Street's shops with the Lyric. We got cones in the summer months to take into the theater. The store kept itself as cold as its ice creams. Mom always got a glass of seltzer water with hers.

Those years walking to the Lyric seemed to go on forever. When I saw the last kiddie show and when I went to the last afternoon or evening double feature, I don't recall. But the Lyric closed its doors one day, and now I play the routines of time spent there in my mind—a film reel of memory.

162 Main Street, Unionville

"We took the bus downtown at Main and Pearl Streets near the bank," Mom said when I asked her how we got to Unionville. She said the bus ride from there to my Aunt Florence and Uncle Frank Cilento's home took about twenty-five minutes without stops. The excursion to Unionville with Mother, Grandma, me, and my sister, Jan, was an exciting trip out of Hartford and into the suburbs for a day.

The bus driver left us off in the center of Unionville at the big and busy traffic circle. The area was pretty with the stone First Church of Christ and Unionville's Soldiers Memorial statue honoring the Civil War fallen. My relatives' house at 162 Main Street, stood on one of five streets that radiated from the intersection. From there we walked Main to their home, carrying what we brought for the day. That walk seemed to take forever but was only ten minutes depending on how fast Grandma walked.

Main Street to my relatives' home was lined on the right with rock ledges and hills, all dotted with myriad trees which followed us to my aunt and uncle's house. 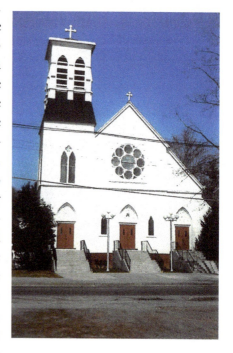 At the end of the long block, we passed the white wooden 1875 St. Mary's Catholic Church with its many steps and three red front door entrances. The section of Main Street from the intersection held sixteen structures and a couple of buildings, including an Italianate and two homes in the same style as my relatives' house. A brick commercial structure bookended one corner of Main near the intersection and St. Mary's the other. Bidwell Square, the cul-de-sac street we crossed to 162, ran along the right side of the Cilento house around its backside and to its left as well. There were eight houses on Bidwell, and no matter where you walked, you could see my relatives' house. We each wanted to be the first to see 162, and I counted to the eighth house from the intersection corner. And then, "There it is!" one of us would say when we spotted the white picket fence surrounding their home. My cousins, Nancy and Donna, would sit on a curb waiting for us, anxious as we for the visit.

The house was bought, according to my aunt, "when Nancy was three or four years old." As Nancy was born in 1940, that would be either 1943 or 1944. Mother said, "Florence and Frank moved to Quaker Lane when they married and to Unionville later." They would live in Unionville for thirteen years. The house was built in 1880 toward the end of the Victorian Era. It included three stories, four if you counted the basement. The house's architecture was never at rest, what with its myriad windows, peaks, and gables. I loved its restlessness.

Their home was beautiful not only out but inside as well. My aunt had good taste and Mother said, "Flossie works hard in that house. It's always spic-and-span." There was a lot of work, what with all of the rooms on each of the three main floors.

The first floor included the kitchen with its open pantry and off the kitchen, a back staircase that went to the third-floor attic. The den had a closet for my cousins' toys and a hand-cranked Victrola, which still worked in the 1950s and looked like the RCA logo with its big speaker resembling a bullhorn. My relatives played some of the old 78 records on it for me. It was an antique even then, and unhappily, when they sold and left the house to move to West Hartford, they didn't take it with them. Also on the first floor was a dining and living room, each with a black marble fireplace. A formal front hall with a staircase to the second floor greeted you from the front veranda.

The second floor had the four bedrooms, a bathroom, and hallway connecting the rooms. The front bedroom and bath flanked a linen closet. Three of the bedrooms had connecting doors. In the hallway, a door led to a staircase to the attic. Donna's bedroom had a door to a hallway leading to the back staircase to the attic too. It seemed all rooms led to the attic. Her bedroom was over the kitchen, and that staircase passed her bedroom as well. In my younger cousin's room sat a special rag doll called a Topsy-Turvy. When you turned it over, its long skirt tumbled down and exposed another doll. I loved flipping it over and over.

The third-floor attic had four rooms. There were two steps into the largest room, and each room was off a small hallway. One of the rooms had a booth that came from my Aunt Millie's restaurant on Park Street. My cousins used the big attic room as their clubhouse.

I loved the doors which went to rooms you didn't expect them to, and several first-floor ones went to front and side verandas, which draped themselves on the house like fine aprons. The back staircases accessed all of the floors. I loved the unexpected, the mysteriousness of the house's busy architecture. It was a marvelous old house and contrasted so to our Hartford flat with its methodical one-floor layout. All our doors led where one expected. No surprises at 119 Hungerford's second-floor flat. I loved my Hartford home, but there was nothing about the architecture that fired a child's imagination. Compared to the active exterior and interior of my relatives' home, our flat was passive.

And the support and lowest level of 162 was its dirt floor cellar. It was creepy, and Uncle Frank made it more so by warning me to never ever go down there. Only he could chance it. It was black looking down into it from the kitchen, and I heeded his warning. I never saw the basement save at the head of its stairs. Grandma, too, had our unpleasant Hungerford Street cellar, but I had no choice but to venture into hers to fill our oil jug.

My Aunt Florence was the youngest of Grandma's six daughters and my mother the second youngest. Both Flossie, as we all called her, and my mother were close throughout their childhood and adulthood, with two years difference in their ages. My cousin Nancy was two years older than me, and Donna, one year younger. Jan was the youngest.

Finally there, we chatted, unloaded the food we brought to add to my aunt's menu, and settled down on one of the verandas or sat in an Adirondack in a side yard. There were lots of fun activities for four young cousins to do in a day. There was the big lot across the street from St. Mary's where we could run around, ride bikes, or just walk. When the church held masses, parishioners used the lot for parking. A black wrought iron fence surrounded the whole area.

About fifteen minutes by bike from 162, there was the huge Unionville Lions pool we swam in, and I recall the green water, so different from Pope Park's sparkling blue color. Lion's pool was fed by a fresh water spring, and the water was freezing. There were water bugs in it sharing the swimming with us. The two sides of the pool at the deep end were steep and had a diving board. I remember Uncle Frank driving Nancy, Donna, and me there evenings. Jan, at the time, was too little to use the pool. Like the procedures set up at Pope Park, we had to shower before swimming. My uncle and I agreed on one thing, and that was everyone, especially one's boyfriend and males in general, should know how to swim. He told me, "Don't go with any fella who can't at least swim!" We agreed that would be a trait neither of us would tolerate. It was a prejudice I held for life.

In Nancy's room, during a visit, she showed me her film star collection. I had, at eleven, begun my own. We sat on her bed, movie star pictures all over it, and the sun tumbled in through the sheer, frill curtains my aunt had on every window. My cousin's favorite actor was Marlon Brando. I liked him too.

It's the nature of recalling long ago memories that one doesn't know how many times the routines that make up a recollection repeated themselves. The final sum of the remembrance comes together to create a memoir chapter as one composite routine, when in reality, many might have made it up. So it was in recalling my visits to Unionville. Memories of those wonderful excursions filter down through the decades and fuse to one.

There is, however, a stunning exception to this philosophical musing. There was a time over six decades ago when no question presented itself but that this particular visit to my relatives in Unionville was unique and would never again be duplicated. It stands alone as one memory. The month was August in the year 1955. I had turned thirteen in February. The journey to my relatives' home this time I made alone. It was the last month of summer vacation before I entered the eighth grade at Burns School. It was on this visit that two other guests shared the time with me—Connie and Diane. They were hurricanes.

Connie arrived first on August 11 and hung around for a second day. She dropped eight inches of rain on Unionville and most of Northern and Central Connecticut and so set the stage for her cousin in chaos, Diane, who followed some days later and finished what Connie had started. Diane dumped sixteen inches of rain in two days. Like a gigantic conduit in the sky relieving itself of an overabundance of water, the countless droplets furiously fused together, coming down in mean torrents into rivers, streams, hills, trees, roads, bridges, and 162 Main Street. The headwaters of the Farmington River rose eighteen inches in twenty-four hours, and a dozen houses along its bank in Unionville disappeared into its raging water. Diane caused the most devastating hurricane in our state since the flood of 1938. No area was hit harder than Unionville with the Farmington River so close. My aunt and uncle, seeing the river rise so quickly and water everywhere, rolled rugs up and put them in rooms upstairs together with small tables, chairs, antiques, and knickknacks. That August, in a little over a week, those two hurricanes dumped twenty-four inches of rain. What a time to visit. I had come for a few days by myself and was in Nancy's room one night as the turmoil outside continued unabated. When the date to visit was selected, no one had predicted the maelstrom in which Connecticut would be submerged.

UNIONVILLE

The family and I were awakened in the middle of the night by a fireman in a yellow slicker pounding the front door and holding a searchlight and bullhorn, ordering us and neighbors to evacuate to higher ground. We piled into Uncle Frank's station wagon. We could have gone to a shelter, but Uncle Frank instead chose to drive to the big hill on Lovely Street. At this point we were unaware of the storm's full magnitude. Aunt Flossie had made peanut butter and jelly sandwiches and took drinks. We stayed overnight in the car and, given permission by the police the next morning, were able to return home. The rain and river water had bookended Main Street, but my relatives' home, in the middle of the street, remained untouched by the river's overflow. The water had come up as far as the business center of Unionville where the bus always let us off.

Others didn't fare as well, and thirteen Unionville residents lost their lives. Homes and businesses were destroyed. The River Glen neighborhood in a low-lying section of Unionville, was completely destroyed. A girl Nancy went to grammar school with spent a night in a tree with her little brother until firemen rescued them the next day. Another young girl my cousin knew drowned, along with the fireman who tried to rescue her. A police officer and a college student trying to rescue a family died too. A horrible helicopter accident killed yet another. And on and on the sad stats went.

The state required an inoculation against typhoid for anyone in the flood area. The line at the Town Hall was long, and I had too much time to think about the needle, the long needle and its sharp point that would pierce my skin and sink into my arm. Too much for me to bear what with everything else so disruptive on this trip, I felt the blood leaving my head and the telltale cold sweat breaking out. I fainted. Dozens of people stood in line in front of me and legions more behind. They watched as an attendant picked me up. My uncle took me back to his home. Sitting in the small den, we all talked and laughed about my fear of needles. This hadn't been the first time I had passed out before receiving one. I was somewhat of an expert by this time. I returned the next day for my shot and, thankfully, got through it standing.

The unrelenting rain was a pounding soundtrack to everything we did. My stay extended. There was no exit over the flooded roads and bridges. Grown-ups were nervous and even kids' nerves frazzled. My cousin, Donna, proved no exception. We sat at the breakfast table in their small kitchen, and she complained that her meal was too dry. My aunt must have been cranky, too, because her retort to the dry breakfast was, "Maybe I should take it down to the river and put it in so it won't be dry any longer." Donna wasn't amused, but Nancy and I were. We laughed, and I'd retell my aunt's reply many times throughout the years.

The storm was serious, but at thirteen, I didn't understand the magnitude of it. I had experienced effects of the hurricanes in the small orbit of my relatives' home on Main Street. I had been there over a week with no electricity, phone, or water. A neighbor on Bidwell Street who had a well gave my relatives what water they needed, and we carried it home in containers. Flossie cooked meals in the dining room fireplace. Eventually martial law was lifted, and the coast guard, police, fire, Red Cross, Salvation Army, and other relief organizations and volunteers left. Without their aid, the death toll would have been higher. Daily life slowly returned to that beloved house and neighborhood of my childhood when a twenty-five minute ride to spend time there with two cousins, an aunt, and uncle, was so eventful, so special.

I would never again return to that home as a guest. My aunt and uncle sold it in 1956, shortly after the flood. They moved to West Hartford.

Several years ago, I revisited the house that had given me so much enjoyment. I walked its exterior and immediate neighborhood. Memory put two sisters back together with their children and Grandma too. We had all lolled in the simple pleasure of visits by bus on sunny summer days with expectation that the tradition would go on forever. Mother took several Brownie snapshots during one of the earlier visits so all of us are in Unionville again, together forever in pictures of that mostly idyllic time.

Dominick F. Burns
Grammar School

I pledge allegiance to the flag
Of the United States of America
And to the Republic for which it stands
One nation under God, indivisible
With liberty and justice for all

And so began each of my Dominick F. Burns Grammar School days for eight years, standing beside my desk, right hand on my heart, and eyes on the flag, the pledge memorized for life.

The school at 195 Putnam Street near Russ was named for the man who dedicated the land upon which the school was built in July of 1940. It's a handsome, two-story, long brick building with myriad window sizes, and it sits on a lawn ringed by trees, all enhancing the beauty of the site. I remember much of my grade school education, which began seventy-two years ago, including the day my mother enrolled me in kindergarten. I was five. And I force those school days to return even if they return in unordered fragments to piece together.

Photographs, documents, and visits to Burns supplement some details in this memoir chapter. The kindergarten teacher, Miss M. Hayes, greeted my mother and me that first day of registration. A tall blond woman, no specific features clear up for a detailed description, but I thought her beautiful. She showed us around the room numbered 116. I felt shy and somber, out of place in the new environment. Mom and Miss Hayes exchanged words and went over the General Information Form that would enroll me as a pupil in morning kindergarten and later in grades one through eight. The school verified my age with my birth certificate. Dad, at his place of employment at the post office on High Street, could be called in case of an emergency, together with Mom's sister, Anna Hamel, or friend Ceil McHugh. A big FINGERPRINTED was stamped in the upper right-hand corner of the paperwork. I began my schooling September 3, 1947. My age—five years and seven months.

The narrow kindergarten entrance turned right onto a larger section furnished with a piano on a left wall and small wooden desks and their chairs to the right. The bay window and glass door at the end of the large room facing Putnam Street revealed a fenced-in playground. Held in with a brick wall, the play area provided a safe haven from the asphalted larger playground at the side and back of the school for grades one through eight. During recess the small area, a chain-link fence embracing three of its sides, kept children in the upper grades from us, and we played unbothered by them.

Those half-day kindergarten classes included routines of orange juice served in small Dixie cups to wash down two squares of saltines and ten-minute rest periods with our arms and heads down on a desk. It seemed the rest time took forever. We sang songs and played games. Not much more was required of us then. Those kindergarten sessions that introduced me to a Hartford public school system ended in 1948. I spent eight more years at Burns.

First there was the plethora of teachers and their differing subjects who came after Miss Hayes and continued the job of educating me. There was the brash Mrs. F. Rosenbaum, my third grade homeroom teacher, who sampled our lunches. Like a grocery market shopper, she checked our lunch bags as we stood in line for recess. I remember the shock when she once slapped my hand with a ruler for talking. Mom was angry but no parent complained in the forties and fifties. As a contrast to her, Miss Olive Cannon, the tottering and shabby-looking old-maid schoolmarm, whose hands shook, was my fourth grade homeroom teacher. She lived on my street, Hungerford, but on the opposite side closer to Russ. She presented a perennial blend of drab grays and tans from her outfits to her hair. She should have retired before I enrolled. But she was as sweet as she was dull.

Mr. Edwin B. Judd served as the school's first principal. Mom said, "He lived on Russ Street way up near Lafayette." He officiated over major and minor events in the school auditorium across the hall from his office and used the curtained stage as a pulpit to announce notices and information. Tall windows lit the side facing the back playground. A plaque left side of the stage facing pronounced "Excellence starts with you." Mr. Judd's portrait hung outside the auditorium and competed for space with the portrait of Dominick F. Burns. In that auditorium I saw a film I recalled all my life because of the lesson it taught about nature.

Filmed on the Galapagos Islands, a giant female sea turtle played the feature role in the black-and-white short. She dragged herself up on shore, heavy with her infant cargo, to lay the thousands of golf ball–sized rubberlike eggs. After laying them, she covered the eggs with sand and left for the sea. She would never see her babies. After freeing themselves of the leathery shell they came packaged in, of the one thousand babies hatched, all but two or three survived the rush to the sea. Birds and sea creatures waited for the tiny feasts. The sea turtle species needed few survivors to continue, and the eaten offspring provided fodder to keep other species going. Nature wrote tough rules. I was horrified and sad.

Art teachers at Burns would never turn me into an artist, and once in an early grade, an art class literally made me sick. It might have been the orange color of the paint, the smell, or a combination of both sensations, but I no sooner began a Halloween project when I passed out as cold as a winter snowball. The nurse called my mother and sent me home early. A nurse would look at me only once again during my eight years at Burns.

The art periods continued throughout my grammar school tenure. Thick primary and secondary paint colors held in tall glass jars had lids tough to turn because of dried paint. We had paint enough to cover every brick on the two stories of the half-block-long Burns School building and used it on two Egyptian art projects. In my sixth grade, Frank Mayock, a new homeroom teacher in 1953, tall, dark-haired, and with glasses, oversaw the projects. The first was a class effort—a mural of the Nile Delta on a huge sheet of paper laid out on the floor. Using bright colors, my classmates and I painted the river a thick royal blue and the sun yellow. A thin green border made do for the vegetation that narrowly hugged the Nile, buffering it from the tan sand around it. It was a beautiful product we had created, and I was proud to have been part of it.

The other Egyptian project required pieces of thick papier-mâché moistened with cornstarch. We layered and pressed the wet mixture against our faces to harden into an Egyptian mask. Lots of fun! Mom bought the ingredients.

Mr. Mayock also introduced us to foreign languages by teaching us Christmas songs in their original French, German, and Latin. I had a crush on him. Today I can still sing *Stille Nacht* and *Adesta Fidelis*, respectively in German and Latin. Had the question of whether foreign languages were spoken in the home on the General Information Form been asked by the time I reached the sixth grade, I could have at least upgraded the answer from "none at all" to "Yes,

Christmas musical favorites." And our cultural education took a step farther when Mr. Mayock oversaw the children's opera, *Hansel and Gretel*. We all took part. I could have, and should have, sung the lead. I had the best voice in the class but was too shy to get up before a full auditorium. This shyness kept me in the choir behind the scenes. The student who got the lead turned to me once during rehearsals and said, "You should be singing the lead with your voice." The cultural exposures to art, language, and opera accompanied me through seventh grade.

There were not only math, grammar, reading, penmanship, and science lessons but home economics as well. Mrs. Mary Scanlon, big busted, tall on thin legs, and who lived across the street from Burns on Putnam, was our teacher. She taught me to make a superb white sauce. The recipe is found on page 56 of the *Outline of Cooking* book used at Burns in the seventh and eighth grades. Once I mastered the few ingredients in it, I poured it over rice, fish—just anything Mother made that would take a drenching in it. Cooking classes converted to sewing in the second half of the year, and I managed to get a straight yellow linen skirt sewn together, which I displayed for a fashion show to an audience of proud mothers, including mine. I would never sew cloth together after Mrs. Scanlon's classes, and I can't cook today. But Mrs. Scanlon told Mom, "Lynn has the cleanest starched and ironed apron in my class."

During those eight years, teachers had a hard time teaching me math. Addition, I got with the help of my fingers, and subtraction seemed doable until borrowing was added. I finally got it. I could be taught through fractions but not algebra or trig. In an early grade, I sat next to Joanne, one of my good friends and the only pupil in school with bleached hair. She lived way up on Park Street in a multi-storied brick apartment block. Once I looked at her math homework paper. If there were ever smaller, neater numbers on a piece of paper, I have yet to see them. I envied her almost print-like miniscule numbers and for a while tried to copy them. I couldn't keep up the effort.

My arm was knocked out of its socket during a dodgeball game on the main playground in back of the school, and a nurse tended me for the second time at Burns. If any injury hurts more than a joint out of its socket, I've yet to feel it. The ball game was part of a rigorous gym program that dressed me and my classmates up in the most awful royal-blue uniforms, which snapped in front and flattered no one, not even a vivacious schoolmate, Linda. But in the baggy uniforms, I climbed the ropes which hung down from the gym ceiling and seemed to reach the sky, jumped the horses, and flung myself around on worn, beige flat floor mats. If I didn't have to shower, it would have been a good part of the curriculum. To have to undress in front of each other, all of us in various stages of development, assaulted my fragile modesty. And Mrs. Shay, with her short, close-cropped curly salt-and-pepper hair, the gym dictator, stood in the door barking orders to "wash, wash, wash."

And school served me not only for readin', writin', and 'rithmetic. It served families as a clinic held on the Russ Street north side of the school. I waited in line with Mother to get my vaccination shots and general checkup. The doctor and nurse used portable equipment, makeshift tables and chairs. They served my health well in those early years, and my attendance remained almost perfect throughout the eight years and kindergarten I attended Burns.

Kids in those seemingly perfect idyllic days of the 1940s and 1950s got bugs, and it was the school's business to make sure they stayed out of our hair. We had checks and stood in line under the five-columned brick veranda on the side of the school beyond the kindergarten play area while a nurse searched through our scalps with small wooden popsicle-like sticks. If you had bugs, nits, or lice, you needed a liquid washed through your hair. It didn't mean you were dirty. You just caught them from someone. But it was like having the plague if anyone said, "She has bugs."

Mom listened, quizzed, and corrected me on most spelling and history lessons. Our favorite spot was in the backyard, sitting in the sun. And when she went to the parent and teacher conferences at night, I waited anxiously for her return with my progress report. She recalled what each teacher said. During the final exercises at graduation in the school auditorium, when I got my certificate of graduation, she said, "I should have gone up with you to share it." She'd say that when I graduated high school too.

Mom rarely packed candy in my lunch, but a store across the street from Burns on Putnam was where I bought sweets for a cent. The store's old wooden-framed screen door squeaked for oil. The store, created out of a residential perfect six structure common in the Frog Hollow, housed people in the remaining five flats on the three floors of the brick building. Not allowed off the playground, I sometimes sneaked across to the store during recess. When I brought candy to the classroom, I hid it under my desk's push-up top. But there was another way to get sweets.

Judith, of 15 1/2 Grand Street, was one of my best pals in those early grammar school years. Her house was on the way to Burns, north side, so I usually picked her up. The half of her house number was because it was built behind 15 Grand. She lived there with her mother, stepfather, and brother. Their rooms were dark and packed with things.

But Judith never left the house for school but that she had a nickel. The nickel bought not only her but me penny candy in a half-story, narrow but long building on Babcock Street that hugged a residence on its left if you faced it. Trees and flanking buildings dwarfed the small structure. The interior, lit by a solitary side window at the entrance, was dark inside. But to Judith and me, it was a candy warehouse of licorice, dots on narrow pieces of paper, Mary Janes, gumdrops, and every other kind of sweet to choose from. If I ever treated her, I can't recall. One morning while I waited for Judy to get ready, her mother showed me a newspaper article about the death of Roy Rogers and Dale Evans' two-year-old daughter, Robin. It was my introduction to a child's death.

There were times when I didn't walk with Judith but rather took a way to school on Park Street passing shop after shop which lined both sides of the commercial and residential street. There was, included among them, the Park Street Bakery where I often bought and ate a five-cent yeast cake on the way to school. The yeast square wrapped in a thin, silver paper with a yellow label slapped on top was as good as the penny candy.

It was with Judith that I played hooky for the first time in the final year of grammar school. We walked up Grand Street near Lawrence one afternoon after lunch and thought it would be fun not to return to the afternoon session. The teacher told our mothers. We gave no good explanation of why we did it but never did it again.

No matter how many clothes in my bedroom closet, I dressed in a new outfit for the first day of each new grade. I got mine from the Youth Center on Main Street in downtown or at Sage-Allen or G. Fox, stores all part of Hartford's premier shopping mecca. My socks always matched at least one color in my dress or skirt. I wore my hair the way Mom liked it, to my shoulders, parted on the left side, and caught with a barrette. It would be her favorite hairstyle for life. I would sometimes have my long hair braided. Powdered Argo cornstarch mixed with water stiffened my dresses, blouses, and slips, and also Jan's, and teachers told Mom, "You have two of the neatest children here." Before ironing, Mom sprinkled our clothes with water which sizzled under the hot iron. The night before school, she hung the outfits on hangers on a wood shelf in the kitchen. Throughout the years, the wire hangers bored tiny holes into the shelf. We owned no television in those years of grade school, and the bright, alert look teachers commented on, Jan and I got at a high price. Mom's rules were strict, and she called us in by six during a school night, and we were in bed by 7:30 p.m. "Lyyynn, Jaaan." I remember playing in the street and her calling us up. The sun hung yet in the sky. Playmates still out on the Hungerford Street always asked, "You have to go up now?"

A picture taken in the first grade presents me in a red plaid jumper skirt, wool, with a white blouse with eyelet trim on the neck and sleeves. Mom was consistent with the same hairstyle for me—parted on the left and caught with the barrette. I missed a front tooth.

One first school day, in the second grade, I wore a red plaid dress decorated with a Peter Pan collar. Mother finished the outfit off with navy socks and the brown-and-white saddle shoes she loved. She kept the white part of the shoes clean with shoe polish, and the challenge was not to smear the white polish on the brown part. A couple of school pictures displayed the same hairstyle and shoes. I took the first day seriously—nervous about new teachers, new classmates, and new classes.

I had a boyfriend early—lanky, dark-haired, blue-eyed Rob who lived on Hungerford Street toward the Capital Avenue end. He had a younger brother, mother, and father—all tall and lanky. Rob liked me right through grammar school. He bought me a doll in a long bride's dress. I have the blond, blue-eyed doll still. I cut her hair short, and the dress, I long ago threw out. He and I went to movies, ate raw potatoes together, and learned to dance in the Burns School gym. "One, two, three, one, two, three." We counted and woodenly stumbled across its shiny waxed floor. His hands sweated and trembled clutching mine as we struggled with foxtrots and waltzes.

And there was the small, blond Walter, who was a close pal during grammar school. We called him Bobby. He was one of few boys who wore glasses. He and his family traveled to Sweden in 1949. We were in the second grade, and I was seven. I presented him with a goodbye note printed on blue-lined yellow paper that might have gone into a Dick and Jane reader:

> Dear Bobby,
>> I will miss you
>> You are lucky.
>> You will see New York
>> You will ride on the train
>> You will ride on a big boat
>> You will see Sweden.
>> I will be glad to see you next year
>> Goodbye, dear Bobby
>
>   Lynn

I used punctuation sparingly but focused on Walter what with nine mentions of him and only three of me. I wrote my name at the end.

And it was the phenomenon of childhood that time seemed longer than it was. I thought summer vacations, which lasted from the end of June to the beginning of September after Labor Day, were a year. I can still smell the new pencils and their woodsy fragrance in the school box we loaded with care. Pencils, erasers, plastic rulers, sharpeners, elastics, and crayons jammed the narrow pencil box space. The box snapped shut in front. One first day of school, Mom bought me a double-decker pencil box with a small drawer on the bottom. She bought it at one of the five-and-ten cent stores on Park Street. I'm pictured with it together with a neighbor in front of my house, and the picture remains one of my favorites as an excellent example of how well Mother dressed me for school.

Jan started at Burns three years after me. I took her to school during her early kindergarten days and introduced her with pride. I was bashful and insecure in grammar school and thought myself homely. Four formal pictures confirmed my opinion. I was getting worse looking by the fourth picture in the 1954–1955 school year at thirteen, when the puberty set in. To me and most other people, Jan was beautiful, and most kids acknowledged her by saying, "She's your sister?"

If there is one conspicuous memory with Jan, it's the day it poured on our way home from Burns by way of Putnam down Park. I put my raincoat on her, and we stopped in Aunt Millie's store on Park Street next to the Lyric where my mother also worked. I was given great praise from everyone there for having given my sister my coat. The compliments for the deed have no parallel in those early years standing near the entrance to Aunt Millie's store as the rain fell. I felt proud and confident.

Mom and Aunt Millie
in front of the store.

The winters piled up snow, creating banks lining Hungerford Street along Russ to Putnam. So high were these minimountains they had to be climbed. And the neighborhood kids and I did. We stumbled and fell our way to school, delighting in the challenge to stay on top. I know there are skeptics who say, "The banks seemed high because you were little then." But I kid you not, they were high. And I stayed up on them until I came to a valley of shoveled driveway and for a moment was ground level again or until one foot collapsed in a soft spot in the snow mound and fell through. One leg up, one down, snow tumbled in to share the inside of my boot with my socks and shoes. The more the challenge, the more fun I had. But the new, white snow turned dark with dirt and other ingredients and finished off with snow plows later in the week. The saying was "Don't eat any yellow snow."

And then there were the wintry days warm enough to turn snow soft and moist for snowballs. On Russ Street near Putnam on my way home after school, a boy threw one that slammed into the back of my head. I never walked home again any winter when I didn't feel the punch of that snowball and anticipate another.

In February, one beloved routine was the buying of twenty-five valentines sold in a box for twenty-five cents. One of the cards was for the teacher. The small valentine cards, most with a red heart somewhere in the design with red-cheeked children, came with envelopes. I took great care and time matching a card to a classmate. I hoped to get a lot and read more into the simple verses than was probably meant. Some cards had no name printed from sender. Each card had a catchy rhyme, and my love of their simplicity persists today by evidence of a collection.

Each homeroom counted about thirty pupils, and a group school picture in the seventh grade was individually reproduced on a 5" × 7" paper with 1/2 inch pictures of us. Dominick F. Burns, Hartford, Conn., our grade, and school year were printed on the bottom. Smiling faces, most boys wearing dress shirts, ties, and even bowties, and girls showing tops of blouses and dresses, looked out from a square. And those years mirrored the Dick and Jane books.

Ninety-three of us went through the Dominick F. Burns Grammar School's grades one through eight. We graduated June 18, 1956. I was fourteen years and four months. The promotion exercises booklet lists my name number twenty-six. We marched into the auditorium to Elgar's "Pomp and Circumstance" and out to Verdi's "Triumphant March" from *Aida*. My mother, father, sister, and grandmother attended the ceremony. I wore a pretty white, fluffy, frilly dress with a wide, blue satin ribbon at the waist and tied in a bow in back. A starched slip puffed out the skirt's bottom ruffles. My hair, cut short with bangs, had subtle curls and waves. Together with lipstick, heeled shoes, and nylons, I felt grown-up even at fourteen. That early June evening was lovely. I had my picture taken in the Hagerty and then the Riccio driveways across the street. The late afternoon sun threw shadows on the ground. I was graduating to a new chapter in my life.

Those were the years at Dominick F. Burns Grammar School when my age went from five to fourteen, from child to teenager. The early formative days consisted of pencils and rulers, chalk and blackboards, lessons and homework, books covered with paper bags held on with tape. They were the eight years of lessons that laid the foundation for four years of high school and beyond. But those later years at high school and college cannot be recalled with the intimate and vivid detail of those earlier grammar school ones. It's curious that recall is sluggish for the recent memories, but it perks and clears up the further back in time one probes. I would change little from youngster to adult. The same sun and shadows of my life formed then, persist today. It is no wonder when so many years later, a grammar school mate can tap me on the shoulder and say, "Lynn, I'd know you anywhere."

> School days, school days,
> Dear old golden rule days.
> Readin' and 'ritin' and 'rithmetic,
> Taught to the tune of a hick'ry stick.
> You were my queen in calico;
> I was your bashful barefoot beau
> And you wrote on my slate, "I love you so,"
> When we were a couple of kids.

Tobacco Summers

I graduated D. F. Burns Grammar School in June of 1956. Shortly after, at fourteen, I would give up my two-month school break to toil in fields. Classmates and I, one spring day toward the end of our last year at Burns, were offered employment in the Connecticut Valley tobacco fields tying, picking, sewing, and hanging tobacco leaves. The opportunity to work was exciting to us as we could earn money for the first time. I'd work to buy school clothes for my freshman year in high school, which began that September. I was thrilled.

The homeroom teacher handed each pupil a parent consent form to take home, fill out, and have signed. My mom never wavered and seemed happy I could fill my summer vacation days working. A few close pals signed up, too, but one, my tap dancer friend, Carol, wouldn't have been able to go had not my mother said yes. I returned the form to school and waited for it to make its way from there through the system of the Consolidated Tobacco Co. which was recruiting us. The company notified us of acceptance, the date to begin after school let out, and where the pickup site would be for my neighborhood friends and me. I'd be part of a generation of young people for whom "working tobacco" would be our introduction to work.

The tobacco outfit.

Mom made my lunch the first day and would every day thereafter that first summer in 1956. She put a sandwich, a fruit, a sweet, and a drink into a paper bag. I'd wear sloppy clothes like jeans and sundry tops. However, Mom still pressed my shirt and pants before sending me off to the bus. What I didn't know till the end of the first summer—no one expected me to last the week. My family thought I'd quit because of the hard physical work in the hot sun. I fooled not only them but myself as well.

I turned right out of my house and walked down Hungerford Street to the corner of Grand, turned right to the corner of Broad to wait for the bus. On Grand, I passed a building where a friend of Aunt Millie had once lived. The pickup point was under a chestnut tree that decorated and dominated that corner with its wide branches and dark green leaves. Now and again it released its chestnuts, still wrapped in their hard-green casings, over the sidewalk. The tree provided relief from the sun while we waited for the yellow school bus in the early morning. The building behind the tree straddled two streets—Broad and Grand. Its address, however, was 48–50 Grand. The building was three-storied, the lower level occupied by businesses, including a key shop. It was an Italianate style built in 1865. It looked great for its ninety-one years. Across the street on Grand, south side, stood a small tavern. There were few parking lots in the 1950s and mostly brick late nineteenth-century buildings occupied all the spaces.

Excited, we waited for the bus that picked us up from the hot July streets of Hartford to deposit us onto the hotter fields of shade tobacco. There were several stops to pick up other Frog Hollow kids and the bus filled by the time it arrived at the field. We kept our lunches in the shade till noon.

Orientation began converting us to tobacco field workers. There were four jobs to do. Two of them for boys—picking tobacco leaves first and later hanging them in the sheds. Under nets, girls tied up the young plants on strings attached to overhead wires to help the leaves climb up and mature. Later, we sewed the leaves in the sheds. The foreman gave us instructions before each new job.

We girls stood under white gauze nets which covered the fields like tropical bedding to diffuse the full sunlight. The humidity produced under the nets from the unrelenting sun, and which made us so miserable, was perfect for the leaves to take from infancy to full growth. The tobacco we worked was called shade tobacco, and the white nets provided just enough to stimulate and coax the growth of the leaves that would cover a cigar with a fine wrapper. The shade tobacco leaf we worked provided the finer, tighter leaf that covered a cigar's first layer. I listened to the foreman's instructions. After a couple of tries, I attached the infant plant to a string that attached to the wire. The predetermined path each plant took made it possible to grow tall and mature in the sheltered light of the July and August sun. Up and down, up and down, I bent to tie, stretched up to fasten. One row done, my ticket was punched to determine my weekly paycheck. I worked slowly at first, faster later as the procedure became routine. Each morning passed quickly and twin problems dominated—being tired and hungry.

Boys and girls all ate at the same time, propped up against a white mesh tent, sandwich bread darkened by hands stained with the leaf nicotine tar or the dirt of the fields. It wasn't possible to totally clean our hands before lunch. At fourteen, I didn't worry about a bit of dirt mixed in with my food. I didn't try to get to know many other kids and stayed with my own friends. My neighbor, Carol, said there was a boy there who had a crush on me, and she teased me.

After the boys picked the leaves off the mature plants and deposited them into large white canvas baskets, our next job would be in the sheds, on machines that sewed the leaves onto long wooden laths before they were hung up for drying. The sewing apparatus was a long table with an equally long row of "fingers" that came round and round. We took two leaves at a time from two piles stacked in front of each of us and inserted them between the two fingers until a lath was filled. We tied one end and put the lath with the ripe long green leaves onto a rack at the end of our station. The number of laths filled determined pay for the day.

Sewing first and later hanging the leaves was done in one of many wood barns that measured twenty by eighty feet. The outer sheds were painted red and of pine post and beam construction, the shed floors were of dirt. It was in the sheds where the curing of the leaves took place. The sheds at least provided relief from the endless summer sun for us. Each end of the shed was peaked, and its huge doors let tractors come and go. Slats that opened on both sides let in air and heat, which began the drying process that changed the fresh green leaves strung up to brown when dry. The slats also let strips of light into an otherwise dark interior.

It was onto one of the wood beams that supported the shed roof where a girl hung the first picture I ever saw of Elvis Presley who had begun his climb to fame in 1956. In the picture, he wore a crass green shirt, had slick, greasy, long, black hair, and looked as tough as the girl who pinned it up for all to see, and I guess she hoped, all to admire.

We were never happier than when we were on the bus going home and our exhausted bodies sank into the cushions. On the way, we did have enough energy to sing mostly one song: "In the Still of the Night." Some sang the words and others the "do-be-do" refrain. The bus driver deposited me and my friends at Broad and Grand under that chestnut tree.

Working on tobacco had physical effects. I became blond again working under the unrelenting sun every day. And I needed no beach to lie on for a suntan. I looked great. Some of my friends got painful tobacco rashes. If anyone could clean the nicotine off during a bath, he or she was lucky because I couldn't. It was only when the season ended that washing and scrubbing my hands countless times finally got the tobacco residue out.

At the end of the season, the foreman hired a driver and we spent the day at Ocean Beach Park. We had a great time. We went on what was called the bullet ride. I was scared and screamed. Seven black-and-white photographs recorded the day. Six of my buddies and I formally posed in differing outfits. I wore a white sweatshirt and dark shorts. We all changed to bathing suits for part of the day to swim in the ocean. The stocky bus driver in her uniform held a cigarette while I photographed her. We had all matured, become confident after working for wages, and were soon to enter high school.

Beating the odds, I survived my tobacco job. I worked that July and August of 1956 and also the two months in the summer of 1957. The routines of that earlier summer mirrored themselves in the next. They were two of the happiest school vacations. I earned $162 the first season and $172 the second. I had, at a tender age, begun contributing toward my Social Security. I had begun to pay for my old age at a young one. I would work another forty-eight years, and each time the Social Security Office sent a record of my accumulated wages, the first two listed were the ones I earned those memorable 1956 and 1957 summers when I "worked tobacco."

Sassafras

I had the first indication in the seventh grade at D. F. Burns School that I might have a writing talent. My homeroom teacher that year, assigned our class an essay. I wrote about our new kitten, Sassafras. We got her about a year before.

Two years before the kitten, our family took in an orange calico stray. She was full-grown when she came to us. We named her Sassafras, Sassy, for short. She was a nice cat, not particularly pretty, but loved ice cream. We had never heard of a cat liking it. But Sassy didn't only have a sweet tooth. When Mom went to the market, the butcher who knew of her cat, gave her small pieces of meat. And so our lives went on for two years with this family addition. Then the day came when a car hit and killed Sassy in front of our home. A neighbor, not wanting us to see her there, had the cat taken away before any of us knew she was dead. My mother and I were told first and our hearts broke. Sometime after, Mom cried when the butcher, who didn't know the cat died, asked her if she wanted a bit of meat for it. She told him of the accident and that Sassy hadn't made it.

It was the nature of neighbors and the neighborhood in Hartford's Frog Hollow during the 1950s, when we looked out for each other, when we felt each other's pain. Given these circumstances, it happened one day in 1954 that our dear friend and neighbor, Kitty Cordner, walked from the end of Hungerford Street where she and her husband lived, to our home. She carried a small box. Peeking out over the top was a kitten so adorable, Mom, who met it first, fell in love with it. The little feline's short-haired fur combined colors of white, gray, and black. Nature had left her beautiful face white. Her eyes sparkled yellow. Mom hadn't wanted another cat after our first Sassy died but couldn't resist this infant. Kitty's brother got the baby from a farm. After having lost our other cat, Kitty wanted to take away the ache in our hearts with this new one. We took her into the family and named her Sassafras too.

It came to pass, not too long after receiving the kitten, I had her on my lap in the living room in front of a book case. I was looking for something to read and sitting on the floor. Soon after, still sitting, I felt a warm wetness on my legs. The tiny feline had chosen to relieve itself on me. She must have felt comfortable and confident to think she could do that. Happy, I wasn't. And from this incident came the topic of the paper to hand in to the teacher. I wish today I had a copy because it was perhaps the first indication I could write. The teacher handed back the other papers but said that she had to read one that delighted not only her but her family as well. She said the essay made them all laugh. It was my paper she read. I was thrilled.

Throughout the years, I took pictures of Sassy but never one as a kitten. The first photograph was my holding her in our backyard. Sassy loved our park-like yard where she spent much time. I often photographed her there, and of the eighteen black-and-white snapshots, fourteen show her in the back, side, or front yard. Sassy was an indoor and outdoor cat and went freely around our home on Hungerford Street. She could be found on the lawn, the front or back porch, or way back in the yard under a flower arbor quite hidden; so dense were my grandmother's flowers. Sassy sat at our kitchen door and mewed when she wanted to go out. She was, however, brought in at night most of the time. Grandma, who lived downstairs on the first floor, kept the bottom door shut. There were times Sassafras couldn't get in so she stayed out all night. I looked over our second-floor porch railing in the morning, saw her on the downstairs one, and said, "Do you want to come up?" She'd look up and mew. I went downstairs to let her in.

Cats are similar in behavior, but everyone's cat has distinct and enduring ways not always duplicated in others. Sassy loved sleeping on my bed and found the spot behind my curled-up legs to settle herself down. First, she'd wait awhile till I was under the covers, peek around the corner from the hall outside my bedroom, and then scurry in, jump onto the bed, and lie down quickly before I could say no. That she scrunched near my legs was okay until I needed to stretch. When I did, I tossed her off the bed. She came back up but had to find another spot around my legs now stretched out.

Mom often woke with Sassy breathing her feline tuna breath in her face. She lay on Mom's chest and looked at her early in the morning until Mom woke and got up. Sassy was hungry, and her meals were mostly Puss 'n' Boots, and she thrived on it for the many years she lived.

But if ever there was a delicacy for Sassy, it was liverwurst skins. She adored them. I'd put the skins in my closed hand, put them near her nose, and in a second she went wild with excitement, anxious for the treat until I released the delicacy to her. At Thanksgiving, she sat in front of Mom's Florence stove oven for hours until the turkey was done. Mom offered Sassy a piece but, as the meat was still hot, the cat had to wait to eat it. Mother would say, "I always give the first piece of the Thanksgiving turkey to Sassy."

Grandma and Sassy

The cat ran the house, and we adored her. She was spoiled and not only picked out the best places to sleep on our beds, but she loved the yard and found places there and also the front porch to loll about or sleep. The neighborhood was quiet and safe, and no fear kept her awake. Even though it was grandmother's house and her yard, Sassy wasn't fond of Grandma who pet her head from the front to back and pushed hard on Sassy's ears. Sassafras squirmed to be released when Grandma, who loved the cat, picked her up. Men made Sassy nervous. It might have been their heavy step or big frame, but except for my father whom she was used to, she panicked, ran, and hid if a man came into our home.

With Sassy under the young willow tree.

Sassy and Mom were pals. It was Mom she met first that summer day in Kitty's box, and it was Mom who was with the cat all day while Dad worked and Jan and I attended school. Mom fed and talked to Sassy and often said, "I tell all my troubles to her." It was to Mother that Sassy brought the praying mantis, birds, and mice she caught, depositing them outside the kitchen screen door. Mom then had to get rid of the catch of the day. I recall once when Sassy hadn't the upper hand—when she threatened a blue jay's nest. The birds swarmed down over and over until she ran away.

One memorable ritual between Sassafras and Mother was Sassy's following her up our street. Mom walked downtown to have coffee and a muffin at Sage-Allen and later shop. Sassy walked after her as far as she dared with Mom telling her, "Go back, Sassy. You can't come." The cat sat awhile and followed a bit more until the street so far up was no longer familiar. She'd return to 119 Hungerford and wait the hours until Mom returned. The two saw each other way up the street. The cat must have looked like a dot that far away. Recognizing Mom, Sassy rolled over and over on the sidewalk, thrilled her friend was returning. She'd roll, then stop and look to reassure herself Mom was indeed on her way, and then roll over again. Mom talked to her from a distance in mock anger, "You bad cat, following me all that way."

Sassy filled our lives for a decade. She died in August of 1964. We lost a dear friend. We would never have another cat. And those sunny days of memory of her and my photographs are what remain. The beloved recollection of the cat and Mom playing out a routine on a sunlit sidewalk in Hartford, companions all those years, remains forever. And it seems in the memory of those days gone by, no clouds mar the recollection, and the sun always shines. I'm left with a sense of loss for what I once had when my life was full and I looked forward to the oncoming years that stretched out in endless numbers.

Sage-Allen

It was the best of times; it was the best of times, those years in the forties, fifties, and later when Sage-Allen and my family did business. The immersion of buildings and people, such a hustle and bustle, it seemed not everyone who showed up on Hartford's Main Street to shop would fit. Sage's stood shoulder to shoulder with myriad big stores and small shops, most built within the nineteenth century. Every building offered a service or product and employed Hartford's people; no gaps, no lots yet from demolition for parking space or modern buildings. The then aging structures were still part of the city landscape.

The tall Sage-Allen & Co. building, earlier called the Hart but by most people Sage's, was designed by Isaac A. Allen Jr., and put up two years before the twentieth century logged in. Nineteenth century architects seemed locked into a see-who-can-design-the-most-beautiful-facade contest. They all get first prizes from me. Run your hand down the front of Sage's, along its rims, over its surface. Double cornices or floral designs, stone garlands and ornate medallions, added for no reason other than beauty, stop you. Arched windows, each with tiny twin columns on them, pretended support. All featured punctilios to enhance the whole. Daring a commercial quaintness rare today, striped awnings shaded Sage's lower windows.

Sage's, crammed on Main Street, was part of a family of buildings wonderfully diverse yet harmoniously integrated. Isaac Allen, without the steel that spawned the later monoliths, made do with the smaller, the exquisite, giving us with this department store a comprehensible sense of place and community.

Residing at 896–902 Main Street, side east, and part of downtown's landscape for so long, Sage-Allen was an old friend. People who shopped in Hartford before me might remember it as one small building on the Kinsley and Main Street corners before two more buildings joined it in 1956. Contractors turned Sage's triple facades into one by slapping on a brick and concrete front, attempting an architectural unity that failed. The addition hid the two short structures and left the Hart building's five top floors exposed. The disastrous face-lift ruined Sage's good looks. Some say the rest of the original nineteenth-century facade languishes under the ugly new face; some say it's gone. The building remains a companion to Hartford's downtown venerable structures. But that Sage-Allen & Co. was an architectural gem isn't the only reason I loved it growing up.

As one of Hartford's retail cornerstones, Mother and Grandma shopped at Sage's. Other Connecticut residents and their kids, teenagers meeting friends, and any combinations of people you can think of shopped there. They came by car; they came by bus. But Mom walked my sister and me from Hungerford Street in the Frog Hollow where we lived, through Bushnell Park, up Gold Street to Sage's most every Saturday. The store and our neighborhood were connected by myriad street routes. The walk took about thirty minutes. There were other department stores to shop in, but Sage-Allen's prices were more reasonable according to my mother and had better sales.

"Hi, how are you today?" said the sales clerks. Personal first, buying and selling second, defined Sage's shopping. My mother even got advance notices on children's clothing markdowns from clerks who advised her: "Why don't you wait until the sale, Mrs. Davis, and get this cheaper?" Sage's was smaller than its major competitor, G. Fox, and Mom found better sales at the smaller venue.

"Sage's has the best year-end buys, especially children's clothes. It's worth standing in long lines for them," Mother said. Many of our Easter and school outfits came from this store.

Mom in a Sage-Allen coat.

And decorating its show windows with clothes and had-to-have furnishings to entice customers in, the store previewed its line like a movie's coming attraction. Sage's contracted the making of its winter coats, so each wore its own store label. Three of mother's wool coats still bear the beige, hand-sewn satin Sage-Allen labels in dark brown script. She couldn't wear the coats out.

And the store's personnel stayed in their jobs long; so long we knew them by name—clerks behind service counters, cooks behind the kitchen's shiny, silver fireproof double swing doors, and bakers whose counter stood near the foot of the escalator that rode us from the first floor to the bargain basement, restaurant, and bakery. I loved riding the escalator and cautiously put my foot out to make sure I had the next step solidly under my feet. The basement restaurant owner, Mr. Fink, ran around in a big, white apron and perennial smile. His conspicuous dedication underscored his investment in Sage-Allen. He sometimes gave my sister and me free cookies, and always asked, "How are you doing?" At the time I was getting cookies from Mr. Fink, I didn't know he owned the restaurant and thought him just an employee. My aunt, who worked in the lingerie department, never doubted how nice Sage's employees were—she fell in love with a manager.

Architecture and shopping aside, the social venue Sage-Allen offered in its unassuming basement restaurant is what Grandmother, Mother, and I loved most, and this eatery was the heart of the department store. Sitting against its restaurant wall, right side from the entrance, at least two dozen framed black-and-white photographs of old Hartford shared my space. It was like eating in a small museum, and I asked Mom, "Where was this, and what's that?"

My mother and grandmother, at different times in their lives, walked to Sage's for breakfast and stood in line with others who ate before shopping. As children, Jan and I had cookies and sometimes hot chocolate, but Mother hadn't money then for breakfast or lunch for the three of us. That splurge would come later for her when childhood was behind me. "Nothing for breakfast tastes as good as Sage's muffins," Mom said. Later in her life, she would go to Sage's for breakfast when I left for work. She walked there, had her coffee, muffin, and cigarette, and talked to other seniors who gathered to eat and socialize. The basement restaurant became an unofficial community center for seniors after my childhood. If you didn't get to the store early, retirees who met there got first dibs on the tables. They talked way after eating breakfast.

It depended on which meal you ate because a friend told me with finality, "My mother and I had lunch in the restaurant on Saturdays when I was little. The chicken sandwiches tasted best." My grandmother pronounced the Boston cream pie slices the superlative food after lunch. I agreed. Cheaper, day-old dessert gave a lot of poorer people a treat they otherwise couldn't afford.

And it was in that Sage's basement breakfast and lunch restaurant that my sister told mother, "You're going to be a grandmother." Mom later introduced her three young grandchildren as she had Jan and me decades earlier, to one of the finest treats—the Sage-Allen chocolate chip cookie. If there was ever a bigger, better-tasking cookie, they have yet to try it. So the Sage's routine was passed down to a new generation.

Our childhood behind us, Mother could decorate and spruce up the flat. Sage-Allen had furnished much of our second-floor Hungerford Street tenement. From the furniture department on an upper level floor, she once carried a pine blanket rack for my room the two miles home. A small end table and matching workbench bought as companion pieces, I drove home. Many of the decorations in our flat displayed the red, script Sage-Allen marker when turned over, including two ceramic soap ball holders in the bathroom and a tin whaler on a pine stand in the living room.

I wonder where the customers went when Sage's was forced to close its doors. Who would have thought it possible, after almost a century in business, for the giant retail to fail, which it did when customers abandoned it and Hartford for malls and suburbs.

And so if buildings like Sage-Allen, where people worked, shopped, socialized, and shared meals, are demolished, if the wares and services they provided aren't needed, then people aren't either. And with every building gone, so, too, goes our physical past—edifices that infuse our memories and create our sense of community. Cities can't survive destroying the structures upon which they were built and thrived.

In later years, this old familiar friend would be restored and used this time as a college. It was a needed step to save downtown Hartford Sage's space that was not only a physical one for me but a personal one as well. The restoration and reuse kept Sage-Allen nestled on its site, remaining there to reinforce my memory of it.

Halloween in a City

It was the greatest show on Hartford's streets in the late forties and early fifties when I was a youngster, costumed and begging for treats in Hartford, Connecticut's capitol city. Festivities began when, making way for the night, the sun went down like houselights in a theater before a performance. The ritual of Halloween was a one-act play, with its unique stage, scenery, dialogue, action, actors, and costumes.

Hartford's Frog Hollow neighborhood streets were the stone and asphalt stages upon which we played out the holiday's mock tragicomedy of tricks or treats. The stores, houses, and three-story tenements provided backdrops to the show. We paraded up and down in front of buildings to enter and exit, blocking in our Halloween play, all passed down from one young generation of trick-or-treaters to another. We had no fear of the darkness or people then. We went out into the holiday night without parents, lugging smaller brothers and sisters with us. No one who opened doors scared us, and Hartford residents, some known, others not, were the supporting cast in our drama.

The Hollow was lit up, including the main treasure trove for goodies—Park—the mile-long commercial and residential street which looked and felt like Broadway that night: lit, busy, loud, and theatrical. The lights of our small white way, from a furniture store, Lincoln Dairy, Lyric Theater, Aunt Millie's store, Delicatessen, and two dime stores, made a mockery of the night, artificially converting the dark to its own manufactured brightness, spotlights showing us the way to treats.

Costumed like a stage performer, I wore an orange-and-black cat trouser outfit topped with a tight-fitting cap. My long, blond hair, despite the cap, squeezed itself out and covered my shoulders like a small shawl. If asked what I was supposed to be, the mean looking feline on the front of the costume, looking like his only repertoire was a prank, gave the answer. I wore a white short-sleeved jersey underneath, and in a light-colored mask, looked like the Phantom of the Opera. Mother bought the costume big enough for me to wear forever. She got it at one of the five-and-ten-cent stores on Park Street next to the Immaculate Conception Church rectory. It must have been déjà vu for the neighbors who, I'm sure, recognized me. I wore the disguise so many Halloweens. My younger sister inherited my cat getup when I outgrew it and she, her clown suit.

The only reason for being out in costume while sunlight still drenched the streets—so Mom could take pictures with our Kodak Target Six-16 Brownie camera that had no flash. One Halloween day, she lined up half a dozen Hungerford Street kids side by side in front of Bill and Ann's house across the street. The Wild West dominated Halloween that year as half my friends wore cowboy or cowgirl regalia of neck bandanas, vests, cowboy hats, and hip-holstered toy guns. The make-believe cowpokes couldn't afford the boots, so Buster Brown socks, saddle shoes, and sandals finished their costumes. My buddies brought the West to the Frog Hollow for a night, the influence of endless Roy Rogers, Gene Autry, and Lone Ranger films we saw at the kiddie show for a dime at the Lyric Theater every Saturday morning.

We carried noisemakers we twirled or blew and wore masks to scare imaginary goblins and ghosts from the night and stake out our streets. Our simple script, "Trick or Treat," required no memorization, no rehearsal, and was repeated at every house and shop doorway. We all had a part in the show and formed a scattered chorus with our one-liner on different street stages throughout the Hollow. Unlike the mischief played out long ago in Mom's day when pails were turned over, mailboxes knocked down, laundry pulled from lines, and soap smeared on windows, ours was a Halloween turned over to children who wanted nothing more than free candy. We waited until dark, long enough for the sun to drop behind the horizon of brick tenement buildings of myriad heights and widths, and then scattered throughout the dense neighborhood hunting for sweets to top last year's haul. We invaded those late October night streets when our ages had one digit.

And there was the bounty—the endless pieces of candy plopped into bags opened like greedy mouths eager for one more. I began collecting the goodies first in my immediate neighborhood of Hungerford, Russ, Broad, and Grand Streets.

There stood on our side of Hungerford at the corner of Grand a small convenience store run by Harold and his wife, Millie, which occupied a small section of a huge apartment block. Mom charged a lot of produce there. On the last day of October, I could go in, get a treat, and not have to say, "Put it on the bill." No look, no pad out for yet another charge penciled in more than crossed out. Not that night.

One tenement on Hungerford Street, other side crossing Grand, second building down, three or four flights up, I recall the lady there who gave us popcorn wrapped in a napkin tied at the neck. Buttered and salted, I remember the goody decades later, unique among so many sweets.

Apples had long been part of the Halloween tradition and also a Mrs. Brown's. She was the wife of the Immaculate Conception Church maintenance man who himself always smelled of spirits, Halloween or not. Tall and big from her knees up, Mrs. Brown seemed top-heavy on spindly legs. She wore her white face powder and thick, red lipstick like a perennial Halloween mask. She was crabby and one Halloween, tossed a wrinkled brown apple on top of my bounty. My friends also got one. We each tossed it away.

Because Hartford was so generous, my sister and I went back home a couple of times to unload our bounty. Mom separated the candy, which she spread out on the kitchen table and then stored in the pantry. She always said, "I don't want you kids to ruin your teeth with too many sweets." Some stuff she threw out.

When I climbed the last stair, knocked on the final door, filled the last bag, when there were no more neighbors to threat with mischief if no treat, I headed with my sister and friends to the Mitchell House, a late nineteenth century two-story public building, for an end-of-the-night party.

It stood at 38 Lawrence Street and was a mecca for the cats, clowns, cowgirls and cowboys, gypsies and ghosts, at the end of Halloween night.

There I gathered with other Hartford trick-or-treaters to brag about how many sweets I got, look over everyone's costumes, and wind down. I lifted my mask, for who cared at the end of the evening if anyone knew who I was. Mitchell House organizers showed cartoons and gave out a few more treats.

But then, this simple pageant of childhood with its one-line dialogue, its display of myriad wonderful costumes, was over. Day's end, a bunch of neighborhood kids had shared the rites of childhood with a city that turned its lights on to welcome and treat us unabashedly well.

I don't remember when I put my costume and mask away for good, pulling down the curtain on another chapter of childhood, but Halloween remains preserved in eight black-and-white Brownie prints and in this reconstructed remembrance.

The Oil Jug

*C*lick, click, click. The sound pierced the night's silence, pushing itself between me and sleep. I was a kid and needed tons of rest. I shut my eyes tight and hoped I hadn't heard it. *Click, click, click.* The sound of the oil jug emptying. Someone had to answer. Couldn't expect my sister, Jan, to get up; she was too young. Didn't Mom or Daddy hear it? Was I the only one the jug screamed out to in the cold winter night in the early 1950s? Was I the only one to have to get up and fill it? The *click, click, click* began to sound like *Lynn, Lynn, Lynn.* No one else stirred. No one but me.

I flung the blanket off and put my slippers and bathrobe on for the trek to the cellar. As if to warn me it was the only source of heat for our big six-room flat, the clicking continued as I took the white jug off its perch in the back of our Florence stove.

The jug stood tall at fourteen inches high, eight inches wide. Its long, thin, curved metal handle had a straight piece at the top for carrying. It warmed my hand. The jug felt light now with little oil in it. I opened the kitchen and hall screen doors, switched on the hall light, and made my way to the first floor. My grandmother, who lived downstairs and had radiator heat in all her rooms, was denied this ritual.

I opened the cellar door. The stout black rubber light switch was located just inside. It took a long turn to catch, but it did, and turned back slightly to hold. It wasn't broken and simply worked that way for as long as I remembered. Despite the hesitancy, it always turned on the bare bulb at the foot of the cellar stairs.

The jug and I made our way down the creaky wooden steps to the damp cellar. The bulb's skimpy light lit up just the immediate area in front of the last step. But I knew where the fifty-five gallon oil drum stood—just to the right of the cellar door to the yard. It hadn't ever been moved from the corner just under one of the small dirty windows that let in a sliver of light to the dank interior. I unscrewed the cap that sat on top of the jug like a hat, put the barrel's pump nozzle in, and pumped the oil to fill it for another night. The brass wire cap spiraled around a nail-shaped nozzle that collapsed to allow the oil to flow when reattached to the stove. The routine so late at night seemed to take forever. I pumped the oil drum handle up and down, up and down, faster and faster. I had to take care not to over pump as I sometimes did, only to have the jug spit out the overfill at me. Sounds in the back of the black cellar were spooky, and I felt put upon down there in the dark bowels of the house. Grandma never put any money into improving the dirt cellar floor and brick walls. The cellar hadn't changed since the house was built in 1897. As I pumped, I looked at the slimy slugs on the damp walls and hoped they'd stay attached. The dirt floor had been stepped on for fifty or so years and was as hard as wood. The damp, dank cellar odor never left, and anything down there for even a short time brought the smell up with it. I once left some movie star scrapbooks down there in a small storage room at the foot of the stairs, and over sixty years later, the musty cellar smell clings to their pages.

I screwed the cap back on, smearing oil on my hands. Up the stairs, I lugged the now heavy jug and set it quietly down outside Grandma's flat, shut the light, and closed the door. I trudged to the second floor and duplicated the door and light routine there.

I held the jug's bottom and eased the nozzle into the perch where it would flow to the two thirsty stove burners that threatened to go out in the meantime. But I always won the race on my shift. The Florence never went out. The small, round, white oil gauge with its silver collar showed empty or full and the words "empty" or "full" could be read, right side up, only when the jug was upside down in its cradle.

I checked the glow through the two small windows in the side of the stove to make sure the oil reached the round felt-like filters. I could also use the large, black stove key that fit into burner tops to check the flames from above. But, as the cast iron stove covers made a lot of noise lifting them up and down, I didn't. Why should everyone be up just because I was. And, even though I scrubbed my hands in the kitchen sink, the smell of oil clung to them. Satisfied the stove was set, I fell back to sleep.

The barrel in the cellar wasn't always filled if Grandma forgot to order oil. One or more local companies specialized in delivering oil, which was actually kerosene, a form of light oil. If she forgot, I had to carry the jug up Hungerford Street past the Cohens' house and the long apartment block to Grand Street to get it filled at Harold and Millie's store. The store's source barrel stood inside a makeshift wooden enclosure built around it on the store's porch. The routine to fill the jug duplicated the one in our cellar. I left the jug on the step before going in to pay or, as was more often the case, to put the cost on our account. "Charge it," I'd say.

Grandma, with her own radiators, never changed our six-room flat from a cold to a heated one. Her oil-burning stove was converted to a Caloric combination gas cooking and heating stove by her grandson and my cousin, Raymond, who worked for the gas company. But it took her a while to get used to the thermostatically controlled unit, and there were times when the heating unit shut off when the thermostat was satisfied with the room temperature. She complained to Raymond. She missed the immediate warmth of her own old oil burner stove and loved ours. She came upstairs often during the winter months to warm her back. The most coveted place in our huge kitchen was standing directly in front of the stove or sitting in the rocking chair next to it.

Sometime in the late 1960s, Raymond took us out of the dark ages of home heating and converted our stove to gas heat. Oil jugs had by then been outlawed in Hartford as they caused too many fires. The jug was removed and with it, another ritual of childhood that involved work and interaction between me and things. I wish I had kept the original jug and the stove-top key.

It isn't in the immediate moment of living your childhood when you realize what you have; it's when you turn back for a look decades later that you wish for one of those days with its rituals of childhood to live over again. Just once more.

Two Stories of Christmas

Mom released our blue Christmas window lights from their tangle of wires and extension cords from a hall closet box. She put them in the front room's bay windows, a signal to the neighborhood the Christmas season in our household had begun. With the help of Scotch tape to hold each on the windowsills, a single blue light occupied two side windows and a companion three-light combination the larger center sill. The lights shone directly across the street to our neighbors, Ann and Bill Hagerty. They were the first to know our holiday season had started.

We often bought our tree during Christmas week because trees sold cheaper then. The salesman, wanting to get rid of as many as possible before the night ended, slashed prices. He sold them in our neighborhood at the corner of Lawrence and Park Street in the Frog Hollow section of Hartford in Connecticut. The week before the holiday, the corner turned into a tiny forest of uprooted firs, pines, balsams, and spruces. Nearby Burns Meat Market and a few other Park Street shops provided the backdrop. Under small, bare bulbs strung out on an overhead wire, the trees leaned against a makeshift wooden fence, built just for the holiday sale. Some nights nature decorated the trees before we did, with a fresh coat of snow no artificial flakes in a bag could duplicate. The Christmas tree stand's lights sparkled against the new fallen snow, and the corner looked like a giant snow globe someone had shaken. With a dollar or two, Mom sent me out to get a tree, which I dragged home.

We set the tree up in the living room to the left of a cardboard fireplace my Aunt Millie gave to us. We thumbtacked our stockings to that lightweight piece with its illusion of a chimney. We hung the stockings with special care in hopes that when heavy with St. Nicholas's goodies, it wouldn't topple.

It took Mom, Dad, my sister, and I to get the reluctant tree in the three-legged red-and-green stand base. The three stand screws to secure the tree never seemed to catch, so our tree often slanted. To right it, we used string and thumbtacks. It looked sloppy but at least stood upright. We prayed it would stand long enough for Santa to finish his work before he turned with a jerk and left for another year.

One year, Grandmother, who lived on the first floor and owned the house, gave us her thin old glass ornaments for our tree. She didn't bother putting one up anymore. Said she had enough of that when her six daughters were little. Mom, my sister, and I decorated. Dad, if the tree was a tall one, put the topper star on. Some of the fragile ornaments didn't make it from one Christmas to another but although broken, could still be used, especially if they had the tiny wire holder that attached them to the tree. We turned those ornaments around so the fractured part faced inward.

And whereas Santa Claus might have had smooth flying because with his eight reindeer he could mount to the sky over obstacles, we didn't. One Christmas Eve, we heard such a clatter, we ran into the living room to see what the matter was. After we had put on all the decorations and the big, red, blue, green, and orange tree lights, Sassy, our cat, playing with the Christmas balls, pulled the tree down. More ornaments were broken, as if we didn't have enough of them hiding broken back ends. The only satisfaction—Sassy must have scared herself out of at least three of her nine lives the way she tore out of the room. Mother bought some of the gifts we got on Christmas morning at one of the five-and-ten-cent stores on Park Street. She sometimes put them on the layaway plan, paying so much a week.

Before Christmas, next to the heat of the Florence stove, Mom read Clement C. Moore's *The Night Before Christmas*. I learned it by heart. She enhanced the story with her own Christmas tale. She told my sister and me about Santa always watching little children to see if they were naughty or nice and the threat of coal in our stocking. For being good, the promise of an orange instead of coal didn't thrill me either. Mother, once we were in bed, put cookies and a small glass of milk out for Santa despite the fact he already had a little round belly and was chubby and plump according to Moore's story. She said Santa needed something to eat because of all the traveling he did delivering presents. I never questioned back then how Santa Claus ever got down any chimney with a bound—even with the magic of laying a finger next to his nose and with a nod up a chimney he rose, let alone our cardboard one.

We lived in what was already an anachronism in our neighborhood—a cold-water flat. We froze in the living room at Christmas, the only time we used the room in December. Mom put a portable heater in the living room and closed the huge mahogany wall doors to the front room to concentrate the heat in the vacuous room. When we went in on Christmas morning, we had on sweaters over pajamas and both under bathrobes. Our breaths vaporized meeting the cold air. We left the kitchen door open to let the heat from the stove escape into the room. I'm sure the heat left the cozy kitchen reluctantly. For a moment, Santa Claus must have been taken aback when he stood in the living room that must have reminded him, as it did us, of the North Pole.

Grandma came from downstairs all bundled up too. We each opened a gift while the others waited. No one opened presents simultaneously, as the time to savor the moment and Christmas would go by too fast. A lot of our friends opened gifts on Christmas Eve. They never thought they might have spoiled Christmas if Santa, delivering their presents, had bumped into them.

Christmas morning, Mom and Dad went into the living room first so that they could watch Jan's and my expressions when we saw the presents, especially the dolls. For a while we forgot how cold we were. The gifts and excitement they generated, warmed us. There was never a wrong guess about what Grandma gave. She gave us slippers every year. I wondered why she bothered to wrap them because the shape of the box always gave any surprise away. I was grateful for everything, even the practical gifts. But I was most excited about what St. Nick took out of his pack of toys for my dolls, Nancy and Mary Jane. I delighted to see them in new dresses, slips, and shoes. I didn't get a new doll every year but only new outfits for the two I had. And those two old friends, with their bright, blue eyes and perennial smiles, seemed delighted too. Once, when times were better, I got a wooden cradle and blanket for them.

Then, just into the New Year, the Christmas tree stood once again, undressed of its decorations and lights. Its needles covered the living room floor. Difficult to sweep up as if reluctant to leave, they clung to the rug.

The warmth of the blue holiday lights in our front room scrubbed out a space in the frosted windows. They peeked out onto the winter nights for a few weeks more, sometimes over a layer of snow the brownstone ledge had caught to adorn the outside and complement the lights.

The stories of Christmas told to me in childhood, Moore's, and the real traditions created by my family, blended together to become one and read over and over again in memory during this holiday's magical time.

The Immaculate Conception Church

The Immaculate Conception Church anchored the corner of Park and my street, Hungerford. The church's steeple stuck up long and narrow into the sky, like an endless finger, pointing to heaven and reminding all of us in the Frog Hollow of our duty to God. The church, built in 1894 at 574 Park Street, was a mainstay for the area and focal point of our lives, where not only praying took place but meeting and socializing with friends and neighbors. We had a sense of belonging.

The church served as a community center whether we thought of it that way or not. And we had the privilege of praying in a setting that was beautiful, what with countless columns supporting a soaring ceiling, stained glass windows, and brass-encased chandeliers. They were memorable decades in the forties, fifties, and sixties when I attended Sunday mass at the Immaculate with my mother, sister, and grandmother. Dad, a Protestant, came on holidays.

My family and I used one of two church entrances on Sunday. We could use a small side one right off Hungerford Street or the larger front one on Park, which we usually chose. Both entry ways sported sturdy brownstone steps leading to massive oak doors. Mr. Sweeney, a church attendant, greeted us and said he always looked forward to seeing our family. We exchanged a few words, blessed ourselves in one of two tall holy water fonts flanking the inside double front doors, and made our way down the right-hand side of the church where we sat. We walked about halfway down, genuflected, and took our seats. We sat in or near the pew numbered 145. Mr. Sweeney not only greeted parishioners, but, if any came late, he then ushered them down an aisle to find a seat, probably quite packed for latecomers. But he usually saw room and had people move in, crunching themselves together. The exceptions were Easter and Christmas. If we or anyone in the parish arrived late, the chances were more than likely we would have to celebrate mass in the basement. It was always cool down there, and the portable chairs setup felt uncomfortable. The altar rigged up for latecomers was small and plain, but served any of us who came late. Besides our confirmation lessons, Mom said that tag sales and other events were held in the basement.

The station of the cross or the magnificent stained glass window near us of John the Baptist baptizing Jesus sometimes provided a distraction for me during mass. In the early years, the stations were beautiful and done in muted multicolors. Later on, thanks to our then Pastor Devine, they were all painted white. I was heartbroken. Expediency and saving expenses also factored into painting over some of the beautiful ceiling works of art, too, with the same white brush during that renovation.

My family and I were joined by other parishioners from streets north, east, south, and west of the church. The Riccio, Cashman, Duchaine, Cherwinski, Hagerty, McHugh, Scanlon, Gerrity, and so many other families came. We were a melting pot of Yanks, Irish, Italians, French, Poles, and Lithuanians who took the time on a Sunday morning to worship. The church held a thousand people, and mostly that's how many filled the pews each Sunday. Five masses were held every Sabbath to accommodate us. The priest looked down upon his congregation from a lovely, ornate pulpit he accessed by several steps. We listened to his sermons looking up. At times a choir and the majestic sound of the huge church organ on holidays or high masses within the unforgettable fragrance of incense, entertained us. Mom liked the early no-frills low mass at 7:00 a.m., as there was no singing and sermons were shorter.

They were the times when people adorned themselves in their best clothes reflecting reverence and respect, worshipping on Sunday. The hats and gloves, dresses and suits, polish and starch said Sunday. But we fussed equally for God as for our neighbors. Mom ironed and starched most of our clothes. She put them on wire hangers and hung them on a shelf in the kitchen Saturday night so as not to wrinkle them. Mother proudly walked Jan and me down the aisle to show us and our outfits off. In each of the long church pews were five hooks for men to hold their hats and women their gloves. The spring-rigged hooks were difficult for a child to open.

They were the times at the Immaculate when it seemed more reverence was shown due to the 1940s and 1950s church customs. On the altar, only the priest and two altar boys officiated at the service, and only they were allowed there. The boys were dressed in a black undergarment topped with a white blouse that stopped at their knees. The tunic sleeves were full and long. Their outfits mimicked the priest's. The young boys responded to the priest in Latin and fetched what was needed during the service and rang the xylophone with a small mallet that ushered in communion. I loved its soft pretty sound. The melody varied slightly, sounding like *dundundun, dundundun, dundundun.* At the end, the boy put his hand on the instrument to quiet the echo. It was an honor to be an altar boy in one's church, and he and the priest remained behind a handrailing that spanned the entire front of the altar to mark the boundary where we lay people could tread. We knelt on a dark red leather-padded cushion as long as the altar rail and, in that kneeling position, received the host. Only the priest dispensed the communion wafer, and one of the young servers held a white cloth-covered board under each of our chins so as not to drop the precious communion. In our church stood many Virgin Mary, Jesus, and other saintly statues, so we had concrete images to pray to. In the early years of my childhood, the mass was said in Latin, enhancing the mystery and separating people from the priest and the mass. We had rosaries to say and missals to read in English.

When attendants passed the long-handled wicker basket around, the church coffers were generously filled for another week to keep it going with our dimes, quarters, and bills, some loose, some in envelopes. Parishioners understood that a church needed not only faith but also money to survive.

My mother and grandmother never had resources enough to have a window dedicated in their names, but some of our neighbors did. The Cordners, McHughs, Dowds, Gerritys, Martins, Riccios, Morencys, and Scanlons were friends and neighbors lucky to have money enough to immortalize themselves with a plaque under one of the many stained glass windows. Mary Scanlon's window, near Mr. Burns's, depicted Jesus showing Mary a heart. Mrs. Morency's showed a girl kneeling near a nun. A tribute for a window with the baby Jesus, Mary, and two men, in memory of the McHugh Family was funded by John and Katherine Cordner, our beloved and long-time neighbors and friends, known to us as Ronnie and Kitty. They made up some of the earliest parishioners who not only attended the church but financially supported it.

The Immaculate never closed its doors during the day in those early years. We could go in to say a prayer or light a candle at any time. The three-tiered metal sanctuary votive holder held twenty-one candles in tall, red glass containers and could be lit with a long stiff wick. There was a slot to insert donations to light a candle. The church accommodated two votive holders, one on each side flanking the front altar. I went in once in a while as a child and recall the clink of the coin as it fell through the slot. The flickering frail candlelight, which comforted me in the quiet, dark church, didn't pierce the vacuous church interior.

Another reason to go into church in between Sunday's masses was for the confession ritual on a Saturday afternoon around three. One priest officiated in the confessional hidden by a heavy, dark curtain. Parishioners, who came in to confess, sat one to a pew and formed long queues waiting to get in to unburden themselves of their sins. It was quiet and the only noise was the opening and shutting of the confessional window when one sinner left and another went in. In turn, the person in a pew moved up and so, too, the rest of us waiting. It seemed to take forever for the line to move. The priest serviced two sides. I spoke ever so quietly so no neighbor heard my confession. "In the name of the father and of the son and of the holy ghost. Forgive me, Father, for I have sinned. I am heartily sorry for having offended thee. It has been such and such a time since my last confession, and these are my sins." The priest listened, leaned toward me, and gave me a penance of this or that number of Our Fathers or Hail Marys to be said after my absolution. I returned to an empty pew at the front of the church, and recited my penance. I felt good having peace of mind and a clear soul. I could now receive communion on Sunday without guilt.

Not only had I a close connection to the Immaculate Conception, but my five aunts and Mother did also. All were married within its sanctuary. I received my first communion and confirmation there. For communion, I had my picture taken in front of the church entrance. It was a formal portrait and displayed me in an almost knee-length white dress topped with a fringed veil. I was as plain as the dress. White polished shoes and socks finished the outfit.

For confirmation I wore a white tunic with a collar that reminded me of clothing altar boys wore. My hair sported braids and bangs. Boys wore a darker costume. I had attended catechism in the church basement set up for lessons for those of us who attended a secular school and not the parochial Immaculate Conception one on Broad Street. My sister and I went to D. F. Burns School, and Mr. Burns, a local merchant and for whom our grammar school was named, funded one of the gorgeous stained glass windows found throughout the church. His window depicted the Angel Gabriel with a sword and a man on the ground. Through him as founder of Burns, we connected to the Catholic school.

Every Good Friday, Mom took Jan and me to the darkened and quiet church just before Easter to kiss the crucifix laid out on a purple cloth near the altar. We each, including Grandma who also came, said a prayer. It was a prelude, a prerequisite to receiving communion on Easter Sunday. All the statues of Jesus were covered in purple cloths until Sunday when they were removed and his exposed figure stood symbolically resurrected into the light and among so many donated Easter lily plants. We, too, were dressed in our finest, and church was a fashion show venue. People were criticized or praised for their Easter outfits. It was only after mass and then breakfast that Jan and I could search for our Easter baskets in our flat under beds, behind doors, and in Grandma's backyard. Neighbors came over to take pictures and have theirs taken in front of our house. So many Easter outfits were frozen in time in those countless snapshots.

The best of times and some of the fondest memories of the Immaculate were at Christmas. A huge nativity set was put up on the right-hand side of a front side altar. No space was spared and everyone connected with Jesus's birth in Bethlehem was represented from the holy family, to the three kings, shepherds, and the animals. Hay, greenery, a painted backdrop with the star of Bethlehem, and palm trees made up the display. The statues were beautiful and the baby Jesus scaled bigger than an infant would normally be. That symbolism was lost on me as a child. At Christmas mass we raised our voices singing beloved Christmas carols. I loved to sing, and I did so loudly. I had a good voice. We left by the side entrance, often from a midnight mass. The light from within the church shone through the stained glass windows to the outside onto snow caught by the wide brownstone ledges. The silent, solemn scene outside seemed religious. After mass, talking to neighbors first, we strolled down Hungerford to a gathering across the street from our home, with our neighbors Bill and Ann Hagerty, their children, and Aunt Ceil. Dessert and drinks were offered, and Ann made a chocolate sweet laced with a cereal that was delicious. I couldn't eat enough of it. We talked, enjoyed each other's company within routines that seemed to go on forever. To be able to relive those early years once again in real time instead of memory, to return to one of those days and have everyone there again, is a recurrent wish.

And then, in 2000, the Archdiocese of Hartford announced that the Immaculate Conception Church, which had served the spiritual and social needs of the Frog Hollow for over one hundred years, would close and convert to a homeless shelter. The inside would be gutted, the pews and organ sold. My heart broke. I used two lunch hours to say goodbye to this old familiar friend. I got permission from the church, which was officially closed already, to go in, say farewell, and photograph. A church deacon let me in by a side door near the rectory. My family and I had never used this entryway. I remained there alone with my memories and camera. I prayed in the pew where we mostly sat, walked the aisles again, and absorbed the magnificent stained glass windows, wood tongue-and-groove walls that lined all sides of the interior, and the rest of the so familiar and stunning architecture that the Immaculate Conception Church and other churches consisted of at the end of the 19th century. I would return a second time and repeat the process in more depth.

I had returned my family, neighbors, and friends, back inside in bygone and nostalgic recollection. I cried. The still solid and saintly church would be another piece of my past dismantled. I would try to walk away from the persistent memories, go forward, but so often turned back to recreate those times through recollection and pictures.

But it's in turning back for a glance at the past, wishing to live it over again but can't, that bruises the heart and soul; and the ache for what once was remains.

Happy New Year

I nvitations to formal social gatherings presented rare events for my family and me when I was a youngster in Hartford. Nevertheless, we were invited to one as regularly and with the same certainty as one year followed another, and that was our annual invitation to a New Year's Eve party. My Aunt Frances and Uncle Joe Del Mastro threw the year-end bash. Fannie, as everyone called her, was Mother's oldest sister. She was usually stern but relaxed and had fun at her party.

Mom and Dad had never learned to drive, so we were picked up by one of four uncles each married to one of Mom's sisters. None of the five sisters ever got a license. Mother, Dad, Jan, Grandmother, and I were the passengers in the vehicle together with my uncle, aunt, and cousins, depending on who had the privilege of carting us that year. We mostly went with my Unionville relatives who had a Woody station wagon.

We left the Frog Hollow in Hartford from our Hungerford Street flat early evening and made our way to 631 Wolcott Hill Road in Wethersfield to celebrate. Every year this event followed our simple but memorable Christmas, and the New Year's party was a nice way to tie in the two year-end celebrations. We were many relatives for the evening, counting among them five aunts and uncles, eight or nine cousins, a few older ones with husbands, and a handful of second cousins. Of course, not everyone showed up. Each relative carried a contribution for the late evening feast, and we dressed up for the occasion, men in suits and ties and we ladies and girls, in dresses and heels. So much was fun and exciting for my family and me, including the car ride, time in a suburb, and being with family and relatives. Something else rare for my sister and me was in the mix at Wolcott Hill Road and that was television. Aunt Frances and Uncle Joe owned one, and I couldn't wait to watch it. But that treat would have to wait a bit. After we arrived, chatted, unloaded mostly food for the meal but also liquor and beer, we walked around my aunt and uncle's cute three-story home they shared with two daughters and a son. As soon as we could, however, Jan and I and a few cousins, plunked ourselves in front of the television airing New York and Hartford's gala city celebrations to welcome in another New Year. One New Year's Eve, with Nancy, my Unionville cousin, we watched *Thing from Outer Space* on the television that was hooked up in the living room. It wasn't long, however, before everyone, including Jan and me, made our way to the basement where we all gathered every year to celebrate the New Year's party.

My aunt and uncle converted their basement to a venue that would accommodate and serve our family, glad to be together again. Portable tables and folding metal chairs joined my aunt and uncle's large permanent wooden ones. Appetizers blended with all manner of foods brought and represented what each relative baked, fried, or just made best. Eating, drinking, and talking created memorable mayhem for hours. The portable tables labored to stand, holding up all manner of pots, pans, and dishes put together by six sisters and their mother, who cooked and baked so well and with enough food for two parties. My cousin Lillian, the Del Mastro's oldest daughter, passed out canapés. Beer and liquor washed the food down for my family, and I'm sure these spirits contributed to the increasing noise as the hours lumbered to midnight.

The basement where our party was always held was a plumber's delight, what with myriad pipes extending from the ceiling and walls, attached to a furnace and air duct, most sporting turn handles of assorted sizes and a few wall meters to complement everything else. Someone had painted the walls anemic beige. Bordered on one wall from the first floor was a wooden staircase with a flimsy outer handrailing that accompanied the staircase to the bottom.

And to complement, trying to make something of the unattractive basement decor, there was an attempt to decorate it with an iron double candleholder, a table with a radio on it, artificial flowers, and a floor cigarette and cigar holder. The large ashtray accommodated the ashes from the stogies Uncle Joe always had his mouth plugged up with. And reflected in the unframed wall mirror, of all things, was one of the huge ceiling pipes. The decorations themselves were seemingly just plunked on the walls, with no apparent effort to coordinate color or unity.

To gild the lily and enhance the family's New Year's Eve gala atmosphere, the Del Mastro family always hung a large, white crepe paper bell together with a red companion one, each held open with a small metal clasp that they suspended from the ceiling where there were the countless pipes to fasten them. Several Christmas cards sat on a shelf and some holiday greens decorated the only window flanked with dull red curtains together with a red wreath in the middle. My aunt and uncle probably held the big party in their basement because no one could possibly ruin it. They were protective and careful of what they owned, even down there, and a large, bulky, plaid cloth-stuffed armchair had a white throw over it. Later in the evening, closer to midnight, we complemented our dressy outfits with all manner of paper hats. No one looked attractive in those head coverings, which Aunt Frances and Uncle Joe provided. The hats were head huggers, all tight at the silver band rim and looser on top. My aunt and uncle had diversified on hats. They came in red and blue, and the silver color was mimicked with a circle on top. Most of us, including my mom and sister, had similar hats, but a few relatives got pointed ones with the same silver trim. They also gave us noisemakers, which tried their hardest to get themselves heard over the noise of at least twenty-five of us, reveling, laughing, talking, and eating. My Irish uncle Jimmy Cassel, handsome with piercing blue eyes and black wavy hair, always teased my Aunt Jenny. He was as bold as she was shy, timid, and shocked by everything. She playfully tried to resist him and keep the mood of the party upbeat. I watched it all as part of the routines played out there every year.

The ingredient for a wonderful party was—too many people in a room not big enough to hold them comfortably. And then, as the hour and minute hands slowly met each other on twelve, the volume of noise ceased for a minute in anticipation of the magic hour striking. And then we all, like a chorus, shouted the one-liner, "Happy New Year." These three words were being shouted in unison across the United States and the world. We turned up our voice volume again, blew into the noisemakers, hugged, and kissed one another with more feeling than usual because we had each made it through another year to greet and begin a new one. Those relatives who were drinking toasted each other. At one point we all danced around in a circle, each relative holding onto one in front, hands on each other's shoulders.

By the evening's end, the tables, cluttered with myriad residual food stuff leftovers, together with the cutlery, dishes, liquor bottles, condiments, cups, and saucers, still labored to stand. What a mess.

Then in the harsh, bright light of the kitchen, so contrasted to the dark basement, we women and girls, still in our paper party hats, gathered to wash, wipe, and put away the dishes. The kitchen had one window with a venetian blind on it and on its wall a rather bright red, checkered print wall paper. There was heightened chatter at night's end, and despite the kitchen being too small to accommodate all who wanted to help, we managed to fit as we did in the basement.

Finally, the long family goodbye. Uncle Frank and Uncle Raymond always said to each other, "We might as well sit for another half hour because it takes the DeMontes that long to say their goodbyes." New conversations began at the party's end and comments on the wonderful evening stretched out the time until we all cleared out.

"Happy New Year! Until next year." The family seemed to remain intact forever, and as sure as the New Year followed the old one, Aunt Frances and Uncle Joe would put on their party again.

The thirteen slides that exist are so grainy and faded, it's almost impossible to recognize anyone. They captured and still struggle to hold the images throughout the years on Anscochrome and Kodak ready mount, all USA made.

The same crepe paper bells are still hanging from the ceiling pipes and are center stage in almost every picture.

Acknowledgments

Chapter 1, pages 7-12, originally published in *Good Old Days, Specials,* January 1999, www.goodolddaysmagazine.com Picture fragment, page 12, *Reminisce.*

Chapter 2, page 17, picture courtesy of M. Martino, Rocky Hill, Ct.

Chapter 7, part of chapter pages 13-20 published by *The Hartford Courant* as Op Ed, December 30, 1997

Chapter 10, page 60, record jackets –"Love Letters in the Sand", 1957, Dot Records, Inc., Hollywood, California, No. 15570; "The Sound of the Crickets", 1957, Marca Registrada, New York, No. EB 71038; RCA Victor Record, "Hound Dog", 1956, No. 47-6604 "Don't be Cruel",1956, No. 47-6604, Marca Registrada, New York, and Radio Corp. of America, Camden, New Jersey,

Chapter 11, page 75 picture of Eleanor Parker and Robert Taylor, 1950s.

Chapter 12, page 79, lobby card, National Screen Service Corp., Universal Pictures, 1956

Chapter 13 page 89, picture in August of 1955 Special Edition of *The Beacon,* The Travelers Ins. Co.

Chapter 14, page 106, Vintage Valentine cards, Airplane is an A-meri
—card x.6544/1 C;

Apple is a CAC 4/5 V2531/1; Fishing is an A-meri-card x.7545 2/ C

And my thanks to Judith Ward, Brian Beaudin, and Rudy Sturk, who took the time to read and comment on the memoir in its earlier stage.

About the Author

Except for close to a decade living overseas in the Middle East, where she worked for the State Department, and Europe, where she taught English, Lynn has lived in Connecticut—the first forty-six years in the Frog Hollow in Hartford. And it was growing up in the Frog Hollow during the 1940s and 1950s that created the inspiration for this memoir of childhood. She currently resides in the shore town of Clinton.

Lynn holds an associate in arts as well as bachelor and master of arts degrees. Now retired, her last positions were administrative at two local colleges. She has traveled extensively and speaks German.

Not only is the author interested in preserving the past with her memoir but is active in preserving the historic architecture of Hartford and Connecticut as well as buildings and monuments in the United States. She holds membership in several preservation alliances.

She has continued writing whether here or abroad and has belonged to writing and poetry groups and participated in writing workshops. She has had essays and poems published.

CPSIA information can be obtained
at www.ICGtesting.com
Printed in the USA
LVHW070219300719

625828LV00025B/1785/P